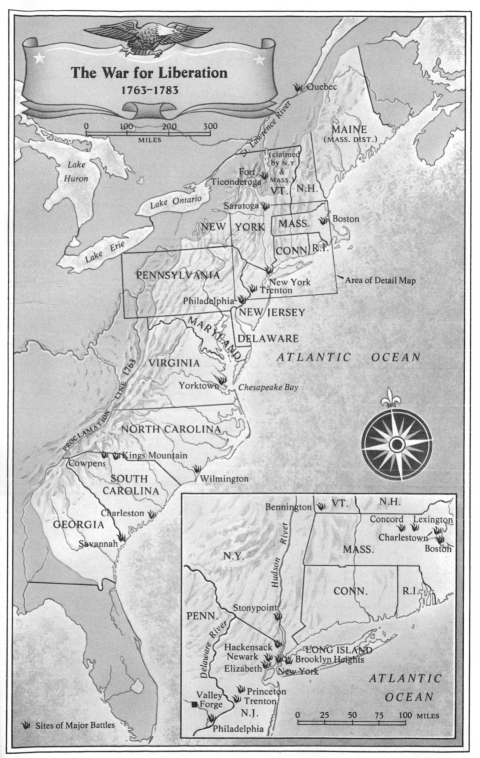

# The War for Liberation
## 1763-1783

0  100  200  300
MILES

Quebec

St. Lawrence River

MAINE
(MASS. DIST.)

Lake Huron

Lake Ontario

Fort Ticonderoga

(claimed by N.Y. & MASS.)

VT. N.H.

Saratoga

NEW YORK

MASS. Boston

Lake Erie

CONN. R.I.

PENNSYLVANIA

New York
Trenton

Area of Detail Map

Philadelphia

NEW JERSEY

MARYLAND

DELAWARE

ATLANTIC OCEAN

VIRGINIA

PROCLAMATION LINE 1763

Yorktown
Chesapeake Bay

NORTH CAROLINA

Kings Mountain
Cowpens
Wilmington

SOUTH CAROLINA

Charleston

GEORGIA

Savannah

Bennington VT. N.H.

Concord Lexington

Charlestown
Boston

N.Y.

Hudson River

MASS.

CONN. R.I.

PENN.

Stonypoint

Delaware River

Hackensack
Newark
Elizabeth

LONG ISLAND
Brooklyn Heights
New York

ATLANTIC OCEAN

Valley Forge

Princeton
Trenton
N.J.

0  25  50  75  100 MILES

Philadelphia

Sites of Major Battles

Map by George Buctel

# The American War of
# National Liberation

# The American War of National Liberation

## 1763-1783

## by Robert Goldston

*illustrated with old prints*

E. P. Dutton & Co., Inc.   New York

*Library of Congress Cataloging in Publication Data*

Goldston, Robert C.    The American war of national
liberation, 1763–1783

Bibliography: p.

SUMMARY: Examines events leading up to and occurring
during the American Revolution. Includes material
written during the period.

1. United States—History—Revolution, 1775–1783.
[1. United States—History—Revolution, 1775–1783]
I. Title.

E208.G63   973.3   76-15156   ISBN 0-525-25546-x

Published simultaneously in Canada by Clarke,
Irwin & Company Limited, Toronto and Vancouver

*Editor: Ann Troy*
*Designer: Meri Shardin*
Printed in the U.S.A.   First Edition
10 9 8 7 6 5 4 3 2 1

*For Bill Moffit and Rebecca*

# Contents

*Illustrations appear on pages 99–109.*

# PRELUDE | The Paths of Glory

*To be beaten is an ordinary misfortune to the feeblest; but the height of misfortune is to be surprised.* —Montcalm

It was as harebrained, foolhardy, and desperate a scheme as had ever emerged from a council of war. But to Major General James Wolfe and the 9,500 officers and men of his command it represented, as one of those officers later admitted, "a last, forlorn hope." For more than three months—ever since June 26, 1759—Wolfe and his army, supported by a powerful fleet, had found themselves baffled by the defenses of the mighty French fortress-city of Quebec, perched on its cliffs above the north bank of the St. Lawrence River. Wolfe's troops had seized the south bank of the river; his Rangers had ravaged the countryside for miles around; his fleet had bombarded the city into ruins. But still the white *fleur-de-lis* banners of the Bourbon kings of France floated defiantly over the citadel while the French and Canadian army of Louis Joseph, Marquis de Montcalm, refused to retreat an inch from their positions beyond the city's walls.

Now it was September and the north winds already carried a touch of frost. Within a few weeks the first snows would fall—to be followed by the appearance of ship-crushing ice floes in the river. But well before the harsh Canadian winter made further campaigning impossible, General Wolfe, his army, and his fleet would have to lift their siege and sail away

| 1

in humiliating defeat. Unless. Unless the mad gamble suggested by Wolfe's three young brigadiers (a gamble in which the general had little confidence) succeeded.

To the military science of the eighteenth century the problem of capturing Quebec seemed almost insoluble. The sheer, two-hundred-foot-high cliffs upon which the city stood made a frontal assault unthinkable. A flank attack then. But where the heights of Quebec tapered down to river level so that a landing might be made (a few miles east and west of the city), Montcalm had established entrenched camps. Wolfe had attacked the eastern camp at the end of July only to meet a bloody repulse; there was no reason to believe an attack on the western camp would succeed any better. Nor could the city be starved into submission as long as it could draw supplies from the hinterland to the north. And, finally, Montcalm's defending army numbered more than 12,000 French regulars, Canadian militia, and Indians—a force far larger than that of the British. Nervous, despondent, and racked by fever, Wolfe had already dispatched a letter to British Prime Minister William Pitt admitting defeat: "I have only a choice of difficulties left," he confessed. His brigadiers thought otherwise.

Their plan was simple. They proposed that four or five thousand men be embarked at night on flatboats from the fleet. These men would row a few miles upstream to a point between Montcalm's western camp and the city itself. They would then scramble up the cliffs, form up on the Plains of Abraham outside the walls of Quebec, and force Montcalm to fight a formal, no-nonsense, stand-up battle.

There were, to be sure, certain difficulties with this plan. If, for instance, the French should learn of the British movement, they would simply mass atop the cliffs wherever their enemies landed and shoot them down while they tried to climb. So Wolfe's four or five thousand clanking infantrymen in their scores of creaking wooden flatboats would have to row up the river in absolute silence. They would also have to enjoy the benefit of invisibility to escape detection by the many alert

French sentries posted along the shore. Nor could Wolfe's men land anywhere they chose; there were only a few places where steep ravines cut into the vertical cliffs so that a man might scramble, hand over hand, to the top. Of course, these places were all well guarded by strong French detachments who wished for nothing better than a target of hapless British regulars struggling up the ravines beneath them.

And if, in some miraculous way, a large body of Wolfe's men should reach the Plains of Abraham in any condition to fight a battle, what then? Then those men would find themselves caught between Montcalm's forces emerging from the city and the thousands of French troops who would surely rush to the scene from their western camp in the British rear. But unless they were simply to admit defeat, there was nothing else the British could do—there was nothing else they could even try to do. So, as he glumly mulled over his brigadiers' desperate plan during the first days of September 1759, it is fair to assume that General Wolfe must often have wondered what unlucky chain of circumstances had led him to his present "choice of difficulties."

A simple answer to that question was not possible. For nearly seventy years England and France had been at each other's throats. During that time they fought four long, bitter wars punctuated by uneasy periods of armed truce. In Europe, where until recently most of the real fighting had taken place, these wars were called the War of the League of Augsburg, the War of the Spanish Succession, the War of the Austrian Succession, and the Seven Years' War. In England's North American colonies the same conflicts were known as King William's War, Queen Anne's War, King George's War, and the French and Indian War—an early indication that to the colonists these European struggles were already being thought of as "somebody else's" wars.

The Bourbon kings of France fought only, so they claimed, to establish "secure" European boundaries for their nation. The English fought, so *they* claimed, to prevent French domination of the entire European continent. As for the French and English colonists in the New World, they fought (when they fought at all) partly because they were told to, partly for land, loot, or fisheries, and partly through mutual fear and ignorance. With the benefit of hindsight we can now see that in North America, at least, all these eighteenth-century wars were really one long struggle to determine who would exploit the fabulous wealth of the American west. But this central fact was not grasped by European statesmen until 1758. That was the year in which William Pitt, the "Great Commoner" (England's Winston Churchill of the eighteenth century), became His Majesty's secretary of state and prime minister.

Pitt inherited a disastrous war. Although undeclared at the time, it had begun with skirmishes and raids in the distant wilderness of the Ohio Valley back in 1754. The French, claiming all the territory north of the Ohio River as part of New France, had built a fort named Duquesne (in honor of their energetic governor general of Canada) at the junction of the Ohio and Monongahela rivers. But the English colony of Virginia also laid claim to this region. In 1754, Virginia governor Robert Dinwiddie commissioned a young Virginia planter named George Washington (he was twenty-two years old at the time) as lieutenant colonel of colonial militia and sent him with 150 men to oust the French trespassers.

Beginning his own personal tradition of military bad luck, young Washington lost the ensuing battle and had to surrender. Since France and England were nominally at peace, the French let the Virginians go home. This was a mistake, for the following year they returned—this time accompanied by the English general Edward Braddock and two regiments of British regulars. Lieutenant Colonel Washington served as an aide to Braddock and attempted to advise the general on wilderness tactics. Braddock, a crusty veteran of Europe's formal battlefields, had ideas of his own. They were wrong, and on July 9, 1755, he led his forces into a deadly French and Indian ambush outside Fort Duquesne. Of the nearly 1,500 officers and men of his command Braddock lost two-thirds killed and wounded; the rest fled "like sheep pursued by dogs," according to Colonel Washington. Braddock died of his wounds, Washington led the survivors home, and the entire Virginia-Pennsylvania frontier was now open to French and Indian attack.

Braddock's defeat was a harbinger of worse disasters to follow. In 1756 this colonial "French and Indian War" merged into the larger Seven Years' War in Europe; England and Prussia versus France, Austria, Sweden, and (later) Spain. Waged on every ocean, in Europe, India, the Philippines, the West Indies, and North America, this conflict was the first truly "world" war—and during its opening years England and her colonies lost badly. The French Canadians captured Fort Oswego on Lake Ontario and Fort William Henry on Lake George. French forces in India captured Calcutta. A French naval squadron in the Mediterranean accepted the surrender of the British-held island of Minorca from Admiral Byng (who was later shot for cowardice, leading Voltaire to remark that the British "kill an admiral from time to time to encourage the others"). On the continent of Europe, England's ally, Frederick the Great, suffered defeat, while the British commander in chief, the Duke of Cumberland, surrendered an entire army to the French. This was the mess that Pitt inherited in 1758.

The new British prime minister turned out to have a natural genius for strategy. While most of his countrymen regarded the fighting in North America as secondary, Pitt made the conquest of Canada England's primary aim. He would send no more British armies to the European continent but let Frederick keep the French occupied there. To the Royal Navy he gave the task of blockading the French fleet in its home ports and convoying British reinforcements across the Atlantic. And he turned over command of England's fleets and armies to younger, more energetic officers. One of these, Jeffrey Amherst, was given over-all command in North America; thirty-one-year-old James Wolfe was assigned to help him. Wolfe, a lanky, round-shouldered youngster with flaming red hair, already had a reputation for both studiousness and impetuosity—he has been called the most Napoleonic soldier in English history. To Amherst he urged: "An offensive, daring kind of war will awe the Indians and ruin the French." The tide of war began to turn.

In July 1758, Amherst and Wolfe, supported by a powerful British squadron, seized the great French fortress of Louisbourg at the mouth of the St. Lawrence. That same year Colonel John Bradstreet and a volunteer force of New Englanders captured Fort Frontenac, where the St. Lawrence flows out of Lake Ontario. At year's end Brigadier John Forbes, with a mixed force of regulars and colonial militia (Colonel Washington was on his staff), finally took Fort Duquesne—which was immediately renamed Fort Pitt in honor of the great war minister.

And then came 1759, still called England's "wonderful year," when every packet boat seemed to bring news of fresh victories. French Guadeloupe in the West Indies fell to a British amphibious operation; Robert Clive destroyed the French power in India; the French fleet was smashed at Quiberon Bay. In North America, British forces seized Fort Niagara, key to the Great Lakes, while General Amherst captured Crown Point and Fort Ticonderoga in northern New York. It remained only for Wolfe to crown this year of victory by the capture of Quebec.

And that was why, in the dark hours before midnight on September 12, 1759, Major General James Wolfe found himself afloat on the dark waters of the St. Lawrence in a flatboat, heading for a desperate venture. He had done all he could to make the brigadiers' plan work; he had chosen a moonless night and found an accessible ravine for his troops to clamber up. He had several transports and frigates sail upstream and down in front of Montcalm's western camp—thereby forcing the French there to march and countermarch to the point of exhaustion. At the eastern camp Wolfe had his fleet open a bombardment and lower boats as if to make a landing—thereby keeping Montcalm's forces east of the city firmly in their entrenchments. Wolfe also enjoyed an amazing bit of luck. It seems that the French in Quebec were expecting a convoy of *batteaux* carrying supplies to slip down the river from the west that very night. French sentries along the shore had been alerted not to fire on this flotilla. Yet the venture remained—desperate. Wolfe, in one of the leading flatboats, softly recited Gray's "Elegy in a Country Churchyard" to a young midshipman, emphasizing the gloomy line "The paths of glory lead but to the grave."

Suddenly, from the shore, a French sentry called out, *"Qui vive?"* The English did not, of course, know the French password for that night, but a French-speaking Scotsman in one of the flatboats replied, *"France!" De quel régiment?"* the sentry insisted. *"De la Reine!"* the Scotsman answered. The sentry was satisfied, and Wolfe's flotilla rowed on. Soon they reached the bottom of the ravine Wolfe had selected. It was called L'Anse du Foulon—but would ever after be known as Wolfe's Cove. Twenty-four rugged volunteers jumped from the lead flatboat and clambered hand over hand to the top of the ravine. There they found a company of 100 French soldiers supposedly guarding this defile. Again Wolfe enjoyed amazing luck—all but a few of the French guards were fast asleep when the British fell upon them. A few shots, a few bayonet jabs, and the cliff top was secured. Back in Quebec, French officers assumed the shots were random—their attention was focused on the fleet menacing their eastern camp.

Now the rest of Wolfe's advance guard—some 1,700 men —struggled up the ravine, their muskets strapped to their backs. As soon as they disembarked, the flatboats returned to the fleet to pick up more men. By dawn on September 13 about 4,500 British regulars, Scots Highlanders, and Royal Americans had reached the grassy Plains of Abraham outside the walls of Quebec. They were formed up in two ranks—truly a "thin red line."

At first Montcalm and his officers had discounted reports that the English were over the cliffs—the cliffs were, after all, unscalable. But as survivors of the guard company from L'Anse du Foulon reached the city, there could no longer be any doubt. Montcalm rushed up troops from his eastern camp —running them double time through the narrow, panic-stricken streets of Quebec and out onto the Plains of Abraham, where they formed up by regiments. The English were obviously determined to fight a formal battle—and Montcalm would accommodate them. He had already dispatched orders to the men of his western camp to attack the English rear. But he could not await their arrival; it was important to attack the British before they had time to entrench. By ten o'clock in the morning Montcalm had assembled 4,000 men. With regimental colors flying, drums rolling, and the men cheering *"Vive le Roi!"* the French attacked.

Wolfe had ordered his men to double-load their muskets and to hold their fire until the enemy were within forty yards. For twenty minutes the British endured a galling French musketry with only the wild skirl of the Scots' bagpipes answering the approaching enemy fire. A shouted command—and suddenly a tremendous roar of musketry crashed into the French advance. A second volley rang out—and a third was not needed. For as the smoke rose, it revealed a hideous carpet of French dead and dying all over the field. Then the English charged the survivors with fixed bayonets (the Scots shrieking their war cries and waving broadswords) to complete the French rout.

Wolfe, personally leading the charge, was shot down. "My soldiers must not see me fall!" he cried. Then, as an officer exulted over the French defeat, "God be praised!" the commander gasped, "I die happy." They were his last words. On the other side of the field, caught in the mass of fleeing fugitives crowding into the city gate, Montcalm was mortally wounded—within a few hours he too would reach the end of his path of glory.

Such was the battle of the Plains of Abraham—described by historians as one of history's "decisive battles," though seldom for the right reasons. The battle certainly decided the fate of Quebec—the city surrendered to the English five days later, on September 18, 1759. With control of this citadel went control of Canada's vital artery, the St. Lawrence River—and so of the Great Lakes, the Ohio country, and all that vast, gloomy, underpopulated wilderness known as New France. More than two centuries later English Canadians would still sing of "Wolfe the mighty hero," while French Canadians nursed an ancient grudge and mourned Montcalm. Yet the destiny of New France had been decided long before these two perished on the Plains of Abraham—had, in fact, been decided by two permanent facts of European geography.

The first of these facts was that England was an island, her people naturally seafaring, her water frontiers secure only so long as they were dominated by English fleets—a matter the English had seen to with great success ever since 1066 A.D. Unmolested by ravaging continental armies behind their "moat defensive," as Shakespeare called the Channel, the islanders had devoted their energies to commerce and civil wars. Commerce meant overseas trade and led, almost haphazardly, to overseas empire. The civil wars, by limiting in turn the powers of aristocracy, king, and church, led to a remarkably high degree of individual liberty and self-government. Commerce and individual liberty led to the emergence of a middle class. The English colonies in North America—originally organized by commercial private companies, largely self-governing, devoted to farming, trade, and personal freedom, and guarded by the Royal Navy—were a faithful reflection of English society.

The second permanent fact of European geography which decided the fate of New France was that between France and the heartland of Asia, aside from a few rivers like the Rhine and the Oder (unimportant obstacles), there were no natural barriers to invasion. The only thing that stood between the French and such unwelcome visitors as the Prussians, for example, was the king's army. Despite more than a thousand miles of blue-water coastline, to France her army would always come first, her navy second. And while Britain's battles were fought on the oceans or on other people's territory, France's battles were fought at home. The maintenance of the royal army, and of the feudal structure which supported it, had been, for the French, more important than individual liberty, self-government, or commerce. The French colonies in North America—established by royal decree, ruled directly and abso-lutely by the king's ministers in Paris, organized along feudal lines, devoted to such limited pursuits as fur trapping to in-crease the wealth of the royal treasury, and guarded by a highly efficient royal army—were also a faithful reflection of French society.

So the English colonies attracted the many who were set-tlers while the French colonies attracted the few who were adventurers. By 1759 there were more than one and a half million inhabitants of English North America, while New France could boast a population of only sixty thousand. New England could, in a pinch, defend itself; New France was totally dependent upon soldiers and supplies from Europe. Once the Royal Navy seriously exerted itself (as it did after 1758) to drive French ships from the Atlantic, the fate of New France was sealed. So Wolfe's great victory before Quebec was more symbolic than decisive—but perhaps that might be said of most of history's "decisive battles."

The Seven Years' War dragged on until 1763. By that time Pitt was no longer prime minister. He'd been forced from office by a new king, George III, who distrusted Pitt's ambi-tions and genius. By the terms of the Treaty of Paris, signed in February 1763, Canada became British. And since France had earlier given her colony of Louisiana to Spain as a bribe for futile Spanish help against England, there was no longer a French presence on the North American mainland. And that fact had consequences which really *were* decisive, if totally unforeseen.

Totally unforeseen? Peter Kalm, a Swedish traveler through North America, had written many years earlier, in 1740: "I have been told by Englishmen that the English colonies in North America, in the space of thirty or fifty years, would be able to form a state by themselves, entirely independent of Old England. But as the whole country which lies along the sea-shore is unguarded, and on the land side is harassed by the French in times of war, these dangerous neighbors are sufficient to prevent the connection of the colonies with their mother country from being quite broken off. The English government has therefore sufficient reason to consider the French in North America as the best means of keeping the colonies in their due submission . . ."

# 1 | The Course of Empire

*What is England now?—A sink of Indian wealth, filled by nabobs and emptied by macaronis! A senate sold and despised. . . . A gaming, robbing, wrangling, railing nation without principles, genius, character, or allies!*
—Horace Walpole

In a very typical, muddled English way it had all been accidental. Britain hadn't set out to conquer the world—only to do business in it. Take India, for example. Certain perfectly normal, conservative, hardheaded merchants had found they could make a large profit selling Indian products such as spices, hemp, and cloth in London. They had sent their ships and agents to that far-off subcontinent to trade. As their business expanded, they had organized, with the government's help and protection, a corporation to finance and direct their affairs —the East India Company.

But India, in the seventeenth and early eighteenth centuries, was a political chaos of petty independent kingdoms, religions, languages, and tribes. Pillage, robbery, and war were constant—and that was bad for business. So, in agreement with local rajahs and princes, the East India Company had undertaken to establish a certain amount of order. They would help in the collection of local taxes, make the roads safe for travelers—that sort of thing. And to do this, "John Company" (as its servants called it) organized a company police force made up of Indians trained and led by company clerks and accountants. This inevitably turned into a private company army.

Nor were the English alone in this; French merchants had

also seen what profits might be made in the India trade. They too had organized a government-protected company which had in turn raised its own private military force. So when England and France went to war, the normal trade rivalry between these companies had naturally and easily degenerated into armed conflict. Both sides soon found themselves enlisting the support of local native rulers and calling for regular regiments from the homeland. When, after half a century of intermittent bloodshed, the English East India Company forces, led by a company clerk named Robert Clive, finally defeated the French, they found themselves the accidental masters of a huge nation.

Or consider the North American colonies as another example. To the religious and political refugees who fled England to settle on the stern and rockbound coast of Massachusetts early in the seventeenth century, the very suggestion that they were the advance agents of empire would have seemed ludicrous and, indeed, blasphemous. Certainly the many thousands of indentured servants, debtors, and convicts exiled to the New World in lieu of sterner punishment at home—the dregs of English slums, the refuse of English jails—had no imperial pretensions whatsoever. As for the Germans, Swedes, Scots, and Irish—these had not braved the perilous Atlantic crossing in order to further English imperial ambitions.

Yet, when the ink dried on the signatures to the Treaty of Paris in February 1763, English politicians were somewhat stunned to realize that they were now masters of a worldwide empire—the greatest empire since the fall of Rome. Furthermore, it was an empire with a difference. Every other empire in the history of mankind had been a tyranny or dictatorship. In this the Spanish Empire was not much different from the Roman or the (former) French Empire from that of Alexander the Great. Absolute monarchs built empires—parliaments did not. When representative governments tried to build empires (as the Athenian assembly and the Roman senate had), they soon succumbed to tyranny at home. This new British Empire would be the first in which the problems of ruling far-off and often alien peoples would have to be solved within the framework of a (relatively) free, self-governing society. English statesmen of a later generation would eventually find a way to accommodate colonial independence, freedom, and the rule of law within imperial bounds by inventing the British Commonwealth of Nations. But all that was far beyond the ken of the men of 1763. In the meantime there was victory, there was worldwide domination, there was wealth abundant. It was all very extraordinary, and the English ruling classes set about enjoying their benefits.

Listen to English novelist Tobias Smollett: "The unbounded riches of the many" afforded "the means of every species of luxury. . . . Clerks and factors from the East Indies, loaded with the spoil of plundered provinces; planters, Negro drivers, and hucksters from our American plantations, enriched they know not how; agents, commissaries, and contractors, who have fattened, in two successive wars, on the blood of the nation; usurers, brokers and jobbers of every kind . . . found themselves suddenly translated into a state of affluence unknown to former ages."

"Gaming has exceeded its own outgoings," complained politician and man of letters Horace Walpole in 1774. "One is tired of asking every day who has won or lost." Charles James Fox, a prominent minister of George III, ran up gambling debts of £140,000—the equivalent of about three million dollars today. Another gambler, said Walpole, "has committed a murder, and intends to repeat it. He betted £1500 that a man could live twelve hours under water; hired a desperate fellow, and sunk him in a ship by way of experiment, and both ship and man have not appeared since."

There were many desperate fellows around—and not all of them were so accommodating. Many became highwaymen. The appearance of these masked desperadoes on the roads around London, armed with heavy dragoon pistols, shouting to halted stagecoaches, "Stand and deliver!" (the "Up against the wall!" of the eighteenth century), became so common an occurrence that most travelers either armed themselves or hired personal guards.

Thomas Hutchinson, soon to be royal governor of Massachusetts, complained of "the dissipated way of life of most of our great men at present." He recorded that the Duke of Grafton (the king's chief minister in the late 1760s) consorted with a prostitute; that the Earl of Chatham was under treatment for insanity and confined in a straitjacket; that Lord Clive, conqueror of India, had committed suicide by hacking open his throat with a penknife.

Walpole wrote of the suicide of the secretary of the treasury, who "could not go on a week longer. The Duke of Athol is dead as suddenly; drowned certainly; whether delirious from fever or from some disappointment is not clear. Two evenings ago Lord Berkeley shot a highwayman: in short, frenzy is at work from top to bottom, and I doubt we shall not be cool till there has been a good deal of blood shed."

Frenzy was certainly at work—even the royal family did not escape disgrace. The Duke of Gloucester, brother of King George III, was banished from the royal court for marrying a woman with whom he'd been living for many years. George III's uncle, the Duke of Cumberland, was sued by another nobleman for seducing his wife. It seemed that of all the aristocracy only the king—plodding, stubborn, conscientious, cautious, excruciatingly dull George III—led a totally blameless life.

The British government in the years following the Peace of Paris was as corrupt as British society. A member of Parliament, elected for seven years, could become extremely wealthy by selling his vote; and the king's ministers were always ready to buy. It has been estimated that by 1774 nearly two hundred members of Parliament were on the royal payroll. Getting elected to Parliament in the first place was also a matter of money. Very few people had the right to vote—only landowners and the wealthy. Some electoral districts, because of shifts in population, had only two or three voters; others were totally owned by one person, who could appoint himself to Parliament if he wished. In some villages the very few eligible voters would join together to sell the local parliamentary seat to the highest bidder. In the larger towns and cities candidates could buy votes for about £5 each. Commoners made newly rich by wartime profiteering and the spoils of empire were willing to pay well for the distinction of belonging to "the finest club in London." A whole breed of seat brokers came into existence who sold memberships in Parliament as a daily business. And however much a seat cost, a new member was sure to recover its purchase price by selling his vote (usually to the king's ministers) on one bill or another; after that it was all pure profit. One honest politician, the Duke of Richmond, sadly confessed: "All I can do, is now and then join with a few others to show the nation, that although but a few, yet all are not sold."

Of course, the great majority of the English people did not benefit from the new feast of empire. For farmhands, tenants, laborers, mechanics, artisans, and servants life remained precarious at best, brutish and hard at worst (which was often). Almost entirely illiterate, desperately ignorant, the vast masses of the poor had no voice in government, no means of altering their fate, which was hunger, poverty, and disease. Wartime inflation only increased their usual distress. The streets of London swarmed with grotesque beggars, prostitutes, half-starved, ragged children, unemployed veterans of the late wars—the disfranchised, dismal multitude. English society was like an iceberg with a tiny, glittering tip and a huge, dark mass submerged in a dank sea of despair.

Yet all Englishmen were supposed to enjoy certain rights. Had they not beheaded one king and driven another into exile to secure them? They had spent most of the seventeenth century fighting to establish a rule of law and "constitutional" liberties. And since this struggle had much bearing upon both the settlement and the development of the American colonies, it will be worthwhile to briefly trace its course.

The turmoils of seventeenth-century England were, basically, the final birth pangs of a new society. Englishmen were casting off the last economic and social fetters of feudalism and, along with them, the feudal concepts of political and religious absolutism. Of course, this struggle had been going on for a long time—perhaps since the barons had forced Magna Carta upon King John in the thirteenth century or perhaps since the merchants of London had begun bartering tax money to the king for increased parliamentary rights and powers in the fifteenth century. The Wars of the Roses, in which the English feudal aristocracy exterminated itself, helped matters along— and so did Henry VIII's disestablishment of the Catholic Church. But the troubles which were to lead to civil war and regicide may be said to have started with the death of Henry VIII's daughter Queen Elizabeth I.

During the seventeenth century Englishmen often looked back upon the reign of Good Queen Bess as a kind of Golden Age, and well they might. For Elizabeth had kept England relatively united, fairly prosperous, and peaceful at home. She did this by ruling with a combination of vigor, parsimony, and toleration. Reluctant defender of the Protestant cause in Europe against the Catholic Counter-Reformation (embodied in Spain's Philip II and his "invincible" armada), Elizabeth yet refused to persecute English Catholics. Though enjoying more absolute powers than any English sovereign was to exercise after her, she yet respected the rights of Parliament. Though requiring ever larger sums of money (especially to maintain the world's largest navy), the kept taxes as low as humanly possible and never levied them arbitrarily. She interfered as little as possible in her subjects' lives and, with wit, charm, and cunning, presided gracefully over England's continuing transformation. She failed in only one respect; she never married and she died childless.

Her successor was James I, son of Mary Stuart, Queen of Scots. Mary, a devout Catholic, had been beheaded by Elizabeth for plotting a Catholic restoration in England. Though Mary's son, James, had been raised a Protestant, men wondered about his sincerity. In this they were mistaken, for

James I took his role as Defender of the Faith (the Anglican faith, of course) much *too* seriously. His wrath was directed against nonconforming Anglicans. These devout people, inspired by the teachings of Luther, Calvin, and Knox, wished to purify the Anglican Church of its elaborate rituals and what they considered its "Popish" decadence.

Elizabeth had tolerated these "Puritans" just as she had tolerated other religious groups. But, since the Anglican Church was part of the state, James viewed nonconformists as traitors and boasted that he would "harry them out of ye lande." He harried out a few—the Pilgrim Fathers, who fled to Holland and thence to America. But in other respects James was far from sincere or even prudent. Coming to wealthy England from impoverished Scotland, he became wildly extravagant. He quickly surrounded himself with a court of mindless glamour boys and ministers who were adept only at flattery. His career of wild spending and scandalous revels had to be paid for by increased taxes. This touched England's merchants, small landowners, and businessmen where it hurt most—in their pocketbooks. Nonetheless, fearful of the kind of bloody civil strife which was torturing Europe, the English people endured James and hoped for better times.

Their hopes were confounded when, in 1625, Charles I succeeded to the throne. Exceeding his predecessor's extravagance, Charles demanded heavier taxes from an increasingly reluctant Parliament and stepped up pressure on the Puritans. Giving heed to Bishop William Laud, a saintly Anglican who viewed all nonconformists as heretics, Charles purged the universities of nonconformists and began jailing Puritan clergymen. Bad as this was, Englishmen suspected even more sinister motives. Charles I's queen, Henrietta Maria, was a Catholic, and both Puritans and regular Anglicans suspected her of wishing to restore the "Old Religion" to England. Finding that Parliament would vote him no more taxes, Charles determined to rule without it and, in 1629, dismissed the last Parliament that would meet for twelve years.

To many Puritans this was the end. Many thousands of

them emigrated to the shores of Massachusetts Bay. For those who stayed behind conditions grew ever worse until, in 1641, full-scale civil war broke out between the king's party (Cavaliers) and the Parliamentary-Puritan party (Roundheads). The fighting continued until 1649, when Charles was caught and executed. Parliament then established a republic, the Commonwealth of England, and attempted to rule alone. But economic and social conditions in England were not yet ripe (nor would they be for nearly two centuries) for the democratic experiment. Parliamentary rule broke down, and the Roundhead army proclaimed Colonel Oliver Cromwell Lord Protector of England. Cromwell ruled as a dictator, but his system did not survive his death in 1658. (His son, who attempted to succeed him, proved a weakling.) In 1660, Charles II was restored to the throne of his beheaded father.

The Stuart kings of England shared one outstanding characteristic—they were incapable of learning from past experience. No sooner had Charles II resumed the crown than he embarked upon the old, fatal Stuart policy of trying to govern without Parliament, spending money wildly, and persecuting nonconformists. That he was not immediately deposed was due, principally, to two facts. First of all, recalling the terrible confusions, mismanagement, and bloody strife of the previous three decades, most Englishmen were unwilling to again raise the standard of rebellion. Secondly, for those pursued too closely by royalist vengeance, there was always the possibility of escape to the North American colonies—now so well established that emigration to them no longer held the terrors it had for a previous generation. The "Restoration" years following 1660 saw a very heavy traffic westward over the Atlantic.

But when Charles II died and was succeeded to the throne by his brother, James II, English patience with the Stuarts finally wore out. Not only did James promise an even greater intensification of Stuart tyranny, but few doubted that he was plotting to re-establish the Catholic Church in England with the help of the French armies of Louis XIV.

Certain eminent Englishmen, casting about for a safely Protestant candidate for the throne, invited the Dutch prince, William of Orange (who had married James II's Protestant daughter, Mary), to "save" them from the toils of Rome. William, with a small army, landed in November 1688, and James II, deserted by all but a handful of followers, fled to France a few weeks later. Parliament, meeting in January 1689, declared that James had "abdicated" and proclaimed William and Mary joint sovereigns. But at the same time Parliament adopted a "Declaration of Rights" which once and for all established its own supremacy over the monarch in the British scheme of government. The Declaration also confirmed to all Englishmen such rights as trial by jury, *habeas corpus*, freedom from unwarranted searches and seizures, and certain other civil liberties—not, unfortunately, including freedom of speech or freedom of the press. This bloodless change of regime (history's most successful coup d'état) was to be known ever after as the "Glorious Revolution." It was all handled so smoothly that it made revolution seem respectable even to the most conservative.

During nearly a century of turmoil much had changed in England. And yet, nothing had changed—it depended upon who you were. Protestantism was now firmly established. Never again would England be threatened by either a return to the Roman faith or bloody religious civil war. But Henry VIII's Church of England, the Anglican Church, remained the official state religion. The various sects into which Puritans had divided (such as Congregationalists, Methodists, Baptists, and so on) would henceforth be fully tolerated—but religion, like everything else, would remain a matter of class. The aristocracy and the very wealthy would cleave to that Anglican Church which was one of the pillars of the state. Lower-middle-class and poor Englishmen might comfort themselves with nonconformist beliefs if they wished. Parliament would henceforth be the supreme governing body of the kingdom; but, as we have seen, only the relatively rich could vote, and Parliament would remain the instrument of the upper classes. As for personal civil rights—there existed no Legal Aid Society in eighteenth-century England. Illiteracy, ignorance, and poverty ensured that the civil rights of the poor would be more honored in debate than in practice.

What had really been going on in England since the death of Elizabeth I had been a prolonged struggle for economic and social power between an older landed aristocracy enjoying royal protection and an emerging commercial middle class. Their differing interests and beliefs had found expression in differing religious forms—as was normal for that age. In order to overthrow the aristocratic-Stuart power, middle-class leaders (sometimes themselves aristocrats with commercial interests) had roused the masses of the poor with the usual promises of a better life and appeals to the "ancient rights" of Englishmen. When it appeared, during the time of Cromwell's Commonwealth, that the poor might take all this seriously—and even proceed to a redistribution of property—the English middle classes were happy to welcome a restoration of the Stuarts. But, as we have seen, the Stuarts remained determined to re-establish an autocratic "ancient regime." Unwilling to once again arm the masses, liberal aristocrats and middle-class leaders (who formed the so-called Whig party) carried out a palace revolution which they then called "Glorious." Basically, what they established was the rule of law in government, in place of the tyranny of individuals—but the law remained what the establishment said it was. Almost every revolution since Charles I lost his head to the axe has followed the same general pattern.

The rulers of the House of Orange—William and Mary, (William III), and Queen Anne—were prudent enough to abide by the rules Parliament had laid down for them, though they were all wily backstairs politicians. Their successors to the throne, the German princes of the House of Hanover, followed suit. Indeed, the first Hanoverians, George I and George II, spoke almost no English, had but little interest in English affairs, and spent most of their time pining for their *Vaterland*. They were content to leave government to the Whigs, who were opposed unsuccessfully during these years by the more conservative elements of the establishment, who called themselves "Tories." Whig ministers generally respected the rights of the king's subjects and even, on occasion, undertook mild reforms to improve the lot of the "rabble." Continuing wars against France and Spain served to generate patriotic unity and also created jobs and general prosperity. The rights of Englishmen who happened to live on the other side of the Atlantic were also unmolested—for they too were heirs of the Glorious Revolution.

But with the ending of the Seven Years' War in 1763 the power of the Whigs came to an end. New times demanded new men. The newly rich (both commoners and aristocrats) who had made their fortunes in the game of empire demanded a government which would protect and advance their interests without quibbling about "Englishmen's rights." They naturally gravitated to the Tory (conservative) party, and in the new king, George III, who ascended the throne in 1760 at the age of twenty-three, they found a natural ally.

Deeply patriotic and, unlike his immediate predecessors, thoroughly "English," George III cherished his empire, his Church, his court, and his wife—in that order. Determined to rule as well as reign, George decided to use the new Tory power to unseat those bothersome older Whig statesmen who were forever admonishing, advising, and correcting him. He sincerely believed in his own divine right to govern. His aim was to create a government of status in which every person, from the highest to the humblest, would have an appointed place. A rigidly aristocratic, frozen society something like that of the ancient Chinese Empire seemed to be his goal. He seldom flagged in pursuit of it. His devotion to daily business was profound, his attention to detail endless, his capacity for hard work unbounded. He was sustained through all adversities by the conviction that he knew what was best for his empire and his people. Those who recognized this simple truth were his friends—those who questioned it were traitors. He saw himself as a sternly benign father; rebellious subjects were wickedly ungrateful children who deserved a hearty caning. They received it, too.

Unrepresented in Parliament by either Whigs or Tories, locked into their poverty, the English masses had no other means of expressing their discontents than by taking to the streets. In 1763 and again in 1768 strikes, mutinies, and riots occurred with alarming frequency in London and other cities. On May 10, 1768, a huge crowd of the desperately poor gathered in St. George's Fields in London. They were protesting the imprisonment of their hero, John Wilkes, one of the very few members of Parliament who tried to speak up for the common people. On the king's instructions the then secretary of state for war, Lord Weymouth, ordered the Royal Dragoons (cavalrymen) to disperse the crowd with exemplary violence. The Dragoons carried out their orders and left six dead and scores badly wounded behind them. This "Massacre of St. George's Fields" was, in effect, a declaration of war upon the lower classes by the king and his supporters in Parliament, who were called (whether Whig or Tory) "the king's friends." From now on dissent would be met by armed force.

And since he was an honestly impartial ruler, there was no reason to believe that George III would deal with dissenting Englishmen anywhere within his empire any more leniently than he dealt with them at home.

THE WAY IT WAS:

*"Friends, if ever we make a plantation, God works a mirakle . . ."*

It was, as the captain never tired of telling them, dangerously late in the year to attempt a North Atlantic crossing. Within a few weeks fearsome gales would begin to blow out of the northwest, and even if they survived these tempests (which was problematical), they were certain to be blown far off course—perhaps into the hands of hostile French or Spaniards, who would hang them all. Furthermore, beating against contrary winds would so prolong their voyage that they might well run out of water, beer, and food and so perish miserably in the dead hold of a ghost ship. Finally, should they somehow reach their destination alive, they would arrive at the beginning of winter, months away from planting time, nearly a year away from harvest. Game would be scarce and fishing dangerous and meager. They would all be dead of starvation before spring.

But the passengers were determined to put to sea. They had unlimited confidence in "ye benevolence of Providence" and, besides, they had no other choice—they were broke. They had invested everything they owned and even borrowed money from London merchants, which would take them many years to repay, in order to purchase and provision their ship. Should they turn back now, they would all wind up in some pestilential debtors' prison. So, despite the croakings and head-shakings of both captain and crew, on September 6, 1620, the ship *Mayflower*, with 102 passengers aboard, cleared the harbor of Plymouth, England, and sailed west down the Channel toward the broad ocean. The passengers, landsmen all, immediately became seasick.

Yet the *Mayflower*, broad of beam, double-decked, with high superstructure "castles" fore and aft, took the waves gracefully. A stout vessel of 180 tons, she was far larger than average in size—much bigger than any of the ships in which Captain John Smith and his company had embarked for Virginia thirteen years earlier. She was also a "sweet" ship, having been engaged since 1616 in the Mediterranean wine trade—although in places she still stank of the fish, tar, and turpentine she'd once hauled from Norway. But, of course, these odors were soon drowned in fouler aromas. As the ship had no sanitary facilities of any kind except the traditional buckets, and as it was not the practice of the time for people to bathe, the air in the narrow, crowded quarters below became nauseating within a few days. Furthermore, passengers and crew had been living aboard for seven weeks before the ship set sail. They'd been waiting for the company of another ship, the *Speedwell*, on the crossing. But the *Speedwell* had proved leaky and, after two abortive attempts to put to sea, had turned back to London for repairs—transferring many of her passengers to the already overcrowded *Mayflower*.

The *Mayflower*'s passengers were a varied lot. Forty-one of them were "Brownists," a sect of Puritans who had left England years before and gone to live at Leyden in Holland, and were now seeking greater prosperity in the New World. Most of the rest were from London and southeastern England. These were not separatists of any sect, but rather members in good standing of the Church of England. A few belonged to the Puritan wing of the Church, but the great majority were quite orthodox. None of the passengers were seeking spiritual freedom in the wilderness (the Leyden Puritans had enjoyed that in Holland), but, like the tens of millions who crossed the Atlantic after them, they sought economic opportunity—a chance to better their lot in this world, not the next.

The passengers were, for the most part, lower middle class, "from the cottages and not the castles of England." But though far from rich, they had been able to purchase a few indentured servants. These, numbering eighteen, had been brought along to do the heaviest labor—to fell trees, hew timber, and clear fields. Their services had been bought for seven years, during which time they would be fed, housed, and clothed by their masters but receive no wages. They were virtually slaves, and were frequently bought, sold, and hired out as such. If the *Mayflower* passengers were fleeing social and economic injustice at home, they were bringing it with them to the New World.

Under luckily fair skies and with a favoring wind, the *Mayflower* sailed through September at her usual speed—six knots. The passengers, crammed into their holds, found it impossible to keep either dry or warm. They rarely had a hot meal—their food was cold hardtack (weevily biscuit), "salt horse" (beef soaked to leathery toughness in slimy brine), stale dried fish, cheese, and watery beer. And, as the weeks dragged by with nothing to relieve the monotony, tensions mounted. The Leyden group despised the Londoners as "idolaters." The Londoners resented the attempts of the Brownists from Holland to convert them. The crew could not stomach the pious ways of the passengers, "cursing them dayly with greevous execrations." One brawny seaman made a point of promising the weak and sick among the passengers that he would bury them at sea. But this fellow suddenly fell ill one morning and died by afternoon. It was, said the passengers, "ye just hand of God upon him."

Then, suddenly, as the captain had predicted, the weather changed. Fierce storms came out of the west, and for days at a time it was impossible to carry a yard of sail. The ship drifted under bare poles, rolling through mountainous seas which threatened to capsize her. Under this pounding many of the ship's seams opened, letting cascades of icy water down upon the ill and frightened passengers jammed below. The storm lasted for two weeks; one of the passengers was swept overboard but managed to hang on to a trailing halyard, "though he was sundrie fathoms under water," until pulled back aboard. Two days later, with a noise like the report of a cannon, the ship's main beam amidships cracked and buckled. Fortunately, one of the Leyden group had brought along a "great iron scrue," which was used to force the broken beam back into place. By this time the crew was threatening mutiny and many of the passengers were in favor of turning back. But after much discussion "they committed themselves to ye will of God & resolved to proseede."

October passed amid successive gales, and on November 6 one of the indentured servants aboard died and was buried at sea. More than a few of the passengers attending the ceremony must have wondered how long it would be before they too were sewn into a sack and committed to the deep. Then, on November 10, at dawn, "after longe beating at sea." the lookout spied a faint, dark line off the starboard bow and cried, "Land, ahoy!" As the excited passengers crowded the rail for a glimpse of their new homeland, one may well believe they were "not a little thankful."

They had missed their destination, which was supposed to be "some place aboute Hudson's river," by a long way. That faint, dark strip of land was the wrist of Cape Cod, and very soon they found themselves "amongst deangerous shoals and roring breakers." Putting hastily about, the *Mayflower* stood out to sea all night. The next morning, more than two months out of Plymouth, she rounded the Cape into what is now Provincetown Harbor—as fine and fair as any on the continent. As the anchor chain roared, it seemed "no marvell if they were thus joyefull." During the next few weeks parties were sent ashore to explore the coast—and mutiny brewed aboard ship.

The mutineers consisted of some of the poorer Londoners and the indentured servants. They resented the authority that the Leyden group exercised over them and had no mind "to serve the turnes of the Adventurers with their travailes and labours." Becoming openly defiant, the mutineers declared that "when they came ashore, they would use their own libertie, for none had power to command them." To meet this situation, certain of the more eminent passengers drew up a "Compact," which they then forced everyone to sign.

"In ye name of God, Amen," the document began. "We whose names are underwritten, the loyall subjects of our most dread soveraigne Lord, King James . . . doe by these presents solemnly & mutualy in ye presence of God, and of one another, covenant and combine ourselves togeather into a civill body politick . . . unto which we promise all due submission & obedience." Although it spoke of "just and equall lawes," as the circumstances of its birth reveal, the Mayflower Compact was intended to forestall rebellion, not to establish democracy.

Six weeks after first landfall, the exploring parties finally decided upon a suitable site. On December 20, 1620, the Pilgrims (carefully avoiding a nearby rock which would have upset their longboat) landed themselves and their scanty provisions upon a sandy beach beneath a hill where they would "plant" their colony of New Plymouth.

But not all the *Mayflower*'s passengers were present upon this happy occasion. One of them, the wife of William Bradford, after staring for weeks at the inhospitable shore with its cold, windswept beaches, its wave-dashed rugged cliffs, its black, bare forest which started at the shore and reached as far inland as the eye could see, rather than endure this "dredful wildernes" committed suicide by throwing herself overboard. Hers was not to be an exceptional case; others in the years that followed were to take their lives when first they saw New England's savage coast. But this murderous land (it would kill half the Pilgrims before spring) was their new home; here they would build "ye kingdome of God."

# 2 | The Grand Tour

*It is no little Blessing of God that we are a part of the* English
Nation.                                                    —Cotton Mather

*I would rather be in dependence on Great Britain, properly
limited, than on any other nation on earth, or than on no nation.*
                                                    —Thomas Jefferson

Emerging triumphant from the Seven Years' War, no more
loyal, imperial-minded, enthusiastic subjects of King George
III could be found anywhere than in North America. Like the
citizens of London, Bristol, and Manchester, the inhabitants of
Boston, New York, and Philadelphia drank bumper toasts to
victory, confusion to all enemies, and God Save the King! Enjoying, in fact, a higher standard of living than most of their
cousins back home, and far removed from the immediate consequences of the king's day-to-day bungling, Americans probably revered their monarch more than Englishmen did. Be that
as it may, the new British Empire was united in victorious
rejoicing and patriotic self-congratulation. And these sentiments, as far as Americans were concerned, were more than
passing; they reflected deep and permanent historical attachments. Ironically, it was the very existence of these ties (of
language, culture, law, and political tradition) which led,
within a decade, to imperial disaster. Had Americans been foreign subjects within the empire—like the Irish, the French
Canadians, or the East Indians—it might have taken them
centuries to rebel.

Who were they, then, these North American English, and
what were they doing on the edge of a continental wilderness?

To answer that question, let us make a tour through space and time. We will restrict our travels to the thirteen colonies which were to become the nucleus of a new American nation; but it must be remembered that they were closely tied to other British colonies which have had a very different subsequent history. New Englanders depended for their livelihood upon the fisheries of Newfoundland; New York merchants developed a thriving export trade in Canadian furs; a South Carolina planter of 1763 would probably have felt more at home in Barbados than in Boston.

Of course, to a traveler of those days such a tour would have been an appalling prospect. Roads were either nonexistent or unbelievably bad—little better than widened forest tracks in most places. They were choked with dust in summer and became muddy bogs in winter. Often blocked by fallen trees or swollen streams, in certain areas they were still menaced by Indian raids. There were no bridges over any of the major rivers, and ferry service was haphazard at best. So bad were the inland communications of North America that the colonies should really be thought of as a string of islands; all important commerce between them was conducted by sea. And for the small wooden sailing vessels of that era coastwise cruising was hazardous and often painfully slow; a voyage from Boston to Charleston could take a month in foul weather.

The frontier of settlement in 1763 left the Atlantic coast near the Penobscot River in Maine, cut across the mountains of New Hampshire to Lake George in New York, ran south through Albany and the middle of Pennsylvania, then hugged the Appalachians to North Carolina, where it again dropped down to the sea. South Carolina and Georgia were almost entirely "frontier" regions, though scattered settlements had been made in the interior.

This settled area of 1763 included about one and a half million souls—of whom nearly a third were black slaves. Within a decade that population was to increase by another million. Most people were engaged in agriculture, but more than 90 percent of the land was still forested. Only near the Atlantic, in areas which had been cultivated for more than a century, could anything recognizable as "farming country" be found; elsewhere farms and plantations were separated by miles of dense virgin forest.

Starting from the Floridas (a swampy, pestilential region won from Spain in 1763, which would remain almost uninhabited for decades), our hardy continental traveler would enter the newest British North American colony, Georgia. Founded to serve as both a buffer against the Spanish power in Florida and a refuge for debtors and criminals by General James Edward Oglethorpe in 1733, the colony almost failed during its first twenty years. This was due to the fact that Oglethorpe and the trustees of his company prohibited both rum and slavery. The indolent sweepings of London's jails (who gave Georgia the highest crime rate of any of the colonies) maintained that they could not survive without both. In 1750 the trustees reversed themselves and allowed both slavery and liquor, but thirteen years later there were still only ten thousand settlers there, including a high percentage of blacks—almost all of whom were engaged in growing indigo and rice.

Continuing north, our traveler would pass through the Carolinas. These colonies (formerly one, they were separated into North and South Carolina in 1729) had been founded in 1670 by certain courtiers of Charles II—among them the Earl of Shaftesbury, the Earl of Clarendon, and the Duke of Albemarle. These gentlemen received their charter by assuring the king that the Carolinas would prove just the right place to grow silk and wine and olives. Considering who the founders were, it is not surprising that they attempted to set up an aristocratic society. There were to be barons, lords, caciques, and even landgraves—whose titles would be based on landownership. There would be a House of Commons, but its laws would require the approval of the nobles. Of course, this scheme foundered immediately under settlement and frontier conditions.

Instead of barons, caciques, and landgraves, South Carolina was populated by poor whites from overcrowded Barbados, a handful of rugged Scots, and, after 1685, a wave of refugee Huguenots (French Protestants) fleeing the persecutions of Louis XIV. Slavery was introduced and, instead of olives and silk and grapes, rice was planted. Because of the malarial climate, planters preferred to leave their inland plantations to slaves and overseers and live an urban life in Charleston, which soon became a thriving port.

North Carolina, on the other hand, was settled almost entirely by former indentured servants and poor whites from Virginia. In their new surroundings they hewed out small farms and grew tobacco, their only cash crop.

By 1763, South Carolina could boast a population of more than a hundred thousand. Charleston had become a gay little city of merchants and professional men as well as absentee planters—it even had a permanent theater. Wealthy Charlestonians sent their sons to England to be educated. But in the interior slaves grumbled and poor whites plotted rebellion.

North Carolina presented a different aspect. Josiah Quincy of Boston wrote: "The number of Negroes and slaves is much less in North than in South Carolina. Husbandmen and agriculture increase in number and improvement. Industry is up in the woods, at tar, pitch, and turpentine; in the fields, ploughing, planting, clearing or fencing the land. Herds and flocks become numerous. Healthful countenances and numerous families become more common as you advance north." Many New Englanders had settled in North Carolina during the 1740s—and they prospered at the expense of the poor "tar heels" of the interior. These numbered nearly two hundred thousand by 1763 and were described by Robert Jones, attorney general of the province, as "bold and intrepid in the art of war, hospitable to strangers, dirty, impertinent and vain."

Virginia (named in celebration of Elizabeth I's chastity) was the oldest, proudest, and most powerful of all the North American colonies. It had been founded in 1607 (Sir Walter

Raleigh's Roanoke settlement of 1587 having vanished) during the reign of James I. Early days had been miserably hard—the colony would probably have perished but for Captain John Smith's friendship with a local Indian chief, Powhatan. But in 1613 settler John Rolfe (who married Powhatan's daughter, Pocahontas) imported tobacco seed from the West Indies. Thereafter Virginia's prosperity was assured. By 1618 the colony was exporting no less than fifty thousand pounds of the weed every year to England, despite James I's warning to Parliament that smoking might be dangerous to his subjects' health. Shredded for pipes or ground into snuff (cigars were smoked only by Spaniards and cigarettes had not yet been invented), the golden leaves became the measure of all wealth —warehouse receipts for tobacco were used as currency. Establishing their plantations along the banks of tidal rivers (for easier loading of bales aboard oceangoing ships), planters preempted vast tracts of land—for tobacco rapidly depleted the soil. They also imported thousands of black slaves to tend and harvest their crops. Later settlers, finding the "tidewater" region already occupied, established their farms in the "piedmont" (French for foothills) of the inland coastal mountains.

By 1763, Virginia's tobacco wealth could be measured in the millions of pounds sterling—but the colony contained no middle class. There were the black slaves, the tidewater planter aristocracy, and the poor frontiersmen of the piedmont. The total population was about four hundred thousand, and, between planters' debts to English merchants, decreasing prices for tobacco on the world market, and the wide gap between rich and poor, plenty of social explosives were on hand.

North of Virginia lay Maryland. It had been sliced off Virginia in 1632 by Charles I and given to his friend George Calvert, Lord Baltimore. Calvert was a Catholic and so named his new colony in honor of the Holy Virgin. He wanted to make Maryland a refuge for persecuted English Catholics (who flocked there by the thousands during Oliver Cromwell's Puritan dictatorship in England). He succeeded in his aim by establishing religious toleration for *all* Christian sects; as a Catholic Proprietor in a Protestant empire he had little choice. Newly made aristocrats themselves, the Calverts established a pseudo-aristocratic manorial system on the banks of Chesapeake Bay. Englishmen of wealth could purchase manors (plantations) and run them with almost feudal dominion over their servants. The size of the manor was limited only by the number of servants its lord could afford. But, as in the Carolinas, frontier conditions soon made a mockery of these privileges.

The plantations of Maryland produced a valuable tobacco crop, but the colony was not totally dependent upon it. Wheat was widely grown, and the town of Baltimore soon thrived as a major seaport. Maryland's population of about a hundred and twenty thousand in 1763 was one-third black—but black slavery was no more important in that colony than white slavery. Without the vast plantations of the Carolinas or neighboring Virginia to exploit, Maryland planters had realized that in many respects the use of indentured laborers was a more efficient and cheaper means of production. For one thing, their purchase price was generally lower than the price of Africans. For another, they could be discharged after they'd worked off their passages or sentences; there was no need to support them in their old age.

As our traveler journeyed north from Baltimore, he found the aspect of the country changing. Entering Delaware (still in 1763 nominally part of Pennsylvania), he noticed that the farms became smaller, more frequent, and better cultivated, the crops more varied. Reaching Philadelphia, he might be as surprised and impressed as was visiting Lord Adam Gordon by such "a great and noble city." Many of its neatly laid out streets were paved and had sidewalks; some were even lit at night (by whale-oil lamps) and policed. With twenty thousand inhabitants in 1763, Philadelphia was the largest and most prosperous town in English America. It could already boast three newspapers (one of which was published in German), a college, three semi-public libraries, the only hospital in North America, and—Benjamin Franklin. The capital of Pennsylvania reflected the solid progress and optimism of the entire colony.

William Penn's "Holy Experiment" had been a success from the very beginning. Unlike most other colonies, it had never undergone a "starving time," largely because it had been organized more recently and could draw its supplies from nearby New York. Pennsylvania had, in fact, been part of New York until 1681, when young William Penn talked the Duke of York into granting him a charter for the southern half of his province. Armed with this and his Quaker faith (the Quakers were a left-wing, pacifist, much persecuted branch of Puritanism), Penn embarked upon one of the greatest real-estate promotions in history. Soon he had thousands of English, Dutch, Swedish, Finnish, and German settlers flocking into his new colony. And why not? Land could be rented for a penny an acre; for £100 you could have a five-thousand-acre country estate *and* a city lot in Philadelphia.

By 1684, Penn could state, without exaggeration: "I have led the greatest colony into America that ever any man did upon a private credit, and the most prosperous beginnings that were ever in it are to be found among us." More than prosperity flourished in Pennsylvania. It was the first community since the fall of the Roman Empire in which different nationalities and religious sects of all kinds lived together in equality before the law. Penn even tried to deal justly and humanely with the Indians, although his agents did put over on the local tribes one of the slickest real-estate contracts in history. This was the famous "walking contract" of 1686. The Indians had sold Penn a tract of land "as far as a man can go in a day and a half," by which they understood a man walking through the forest. But the Pennsylvanians cleared a good trail and then hired the three fastest runners in the colony. Thirty-six hours later, to the disgust of the Indians, the Penn family owned another half million acres of their cornfields and hunting grounds.

By 1763, Pennsylvania had a population of nearly three hundred thousand—few of whom were black slaves, since slavery was frowned upon by Quakers. In any event, the colony's small-farm and manufacturing economy left little scope for the south's "peculiar institution." About half the inhabitants were German, half English. As in other colonies, the western frontiersmen grumbled about the rule of "eastern oligarchs"—with some justification.

Continuing northward meant ferrying over the Delaware River to Trenton and then proceeding across the province of New Jersey. This colony, like Pennsylvania, had originally been part of the huge region granted by Charles II to his brother, the Duke of York. But in 1664 the duke made a gift of it to Sir George Carteret and Lord John Berkeley. When the Carterets arrived to take possession, they found several hundred Dutchmen from New York and a handful of New Englanders tilling small farms there. The new Proprietors then issued their "Concessions and Agreements," which promised freedom of conscience, representative government, and large land grants to all settlers. As in Pennsylvania, this program worked. By 1763, New Jersey could boast a population of more than a hundred thousand, a college (Princeton, founded in 1746), and Nassau Hall—the largest building in English America. A countryside of small, flourishing farms and a seacoast dotted with fishing villages made Jerseyites seem "the most Esie and happy people of any collony in North America." The Carterets did very well in their real-estate business; their descendants are still selling land in New Jersey today.

Crossing the Hudson at Perth Amboy, our intrepid traveler would reach New York City—a compact little town, third in population in the English colonies, still bearing marks of its Dutch origins. These went back to the voyage of Henry Hudson, an Englishman in Dutch employ, who in 1609 first sailed up the river which bears his name. In 1621 the Dutch West India Company was organized, and it founded fur-trading posts at Fort Orange (Albany) in 1624 and New Amsterdam (New York City) in 1626. It was upon this occasion that the company purchased Manhattan Island from a tribe of Indians for some twenty-four dollars' worth of trading junk—a deal over which white men smirked for centuries until recent research revealed that the Indians thus "suckered" had no right to sell the island in the first place (they just happened to be passing through).

The trading post of New Amsterdam began to encourage regular settlement in 1630 under semi-feudal terms. Huge patroonships (grants of many thousands of acres of land) were allowed to wealthy families. They, in turn, could lease their lands to sharecropping tenant farmers, over whom they exercised both civil and criminal jurisdiction. This land tenure system made for constant trouble between the Hudson Valley patroons, who controlled the colonial government, and the farmers and artisans, who thought they'd left feudalism behind them in Europe. The successive Dutch governors of the colony, whom Washington Irving was to portray as comic figures, were actually petty autocrats who governed with an iron fist and mishandled almost everything. The last of these governors, peg-legged Peter Stuyvesant, ruled so strictly that even the wealthy patroons protested his harsh measures. It was not surprising, then, that when England and Holland went to war and an English fleet appeared off Manhattan Island in 1664, Stuyvesant could find almost no one willing to defend the place. He surrendered without firing a shot, and New Amsterdam passed into the hands of the Duke of York, who promptly renamed it in his own honor. In a later war New York was recaptured by the Dutch (in 1673) but returned to England a year later at the peace conference.

The English continued the Dutch patroonship system, modified only slightly to allow certain civil liberties to the English settlers who now flocked to the colony. New York was to remain an oligarchy ruled by the rich until well into the nineteenth century. By 1763 the colony had more than two hundred thousand inhabitants, of whom about ten thousand lived in New York City—a cosmopolitan town which already in-

cluded enough Irish to celebrate St. Patrick's Day, enough
Jews to maintain a synagogue, enough Germans to maintain
four German-language churches, plenty of Dutch descendants
of the original founders, as well as Scots, Swedes, Finns, Ital-
ians, French, and, of course, English. While there were more
black slaves in New York than in all the New England colonies
combined, there were also a substantial number of free blacks,
living, along with Irish dockworkers, in evil waterfront slums.
City dwellers already grumbled about their taxes going to support the upstate farmers around Albany, and these, in turn,
suspected New Yorkers of libertarian sentiments and de-
pravity.

New England, including the colonies of Connecticut,
Rhode Island, Massachusetts, and New Hampshire, was, on
the other hand, racially homogeneous and relatively democratic; almost every adult white male had the vote. The flourishing colony of Massachusetts had not grown from the Pilgrim
settlement at Plymouth, but rather from the great Puritan
migration of the 1630s—during the time of Charles I's oppressions. Buying up the stock of the Plymouth Company, English
Puritans formed a new Massachusetts Bay Company, and in
1630 some fifteen ships carrying more than a thousand settlers
arrived off Cape Cod. By 1634, with royal despotism growing
ever more stringent at home, more than ten thousand Puritans
had migrated to New England. There they established, at
Salem, Boston, Marblehead, and other seacoast towns, a
strange blend of democracy and theocratic dictatorship. Almost everyone could vote—provided he remained a member in
good standing of his Congregational church (the only denomination permitted). The laws were equitable and impartially
applied—but they included all sorts of enforcements of Puritan
religious and moral doctrine. A "Body of Liberties" enacted
in 1641 guaranteed almost all civil rights—except freedom of
worship.

As the population of the Bay area rapidly increased, some
settlers began to feel overcrowded. Declaring that "the bent of

their spirits" required new surroundings, they headed west
(the first such westward migration in American history) into
the Connecticut Valley. There they established three towns:
Hartford, Windsor, and Wethersfield. These became the nucleus of a new colony—Connecticut.

Rebelling against the religious tyranny of the Massachusetts authorities, another group of dissident Puritans, led by
preacher Roger Williams, began clamoring for freedom of worship. They were promptly expelled as troublemakers by the
Bay Colony hierarchy and, after severe hardships, wound up
on the shores of Narragansett Bay. There they built the town
of Providence, and, in 1644, received a charter from Parliament which established their settlement as the colony of Rhode
Island. Advocating complete freedom of conscience, Roger
Williams made the colony a refuge for the disaffected and persecuted from all over North America. More remarkable still, he
maintained permanently good relations with local Indian
tribes, whose languages and ways he studied and whose ancient
customs he carefully respected.

New Hampshire, settled largely by pioneers from the
original New England colonies, was first detached from Massachusetts by Charles II, who gave the region as a personal gift
to one Captain John Mason. But finding it next to impossible
to extract a profit from his wild and mountainous domain,
Mason eventually sold out to the crown, which, in turn, made it
into an independent colony.

By 1763, Boston could boast a population of more than
seventeen thousand, and there were more than a dozen New
England coastal towns, each prospering from some maritime
specialty. Nantucket Islanders chased whales in the Pacific;
Portsmouth exported lumber and spars for England's merchant
marine; Gloucestermen harvested fish off Newfoundland's
Grand Bank; Salem ships sailed the Mediterranean; New Lon-
don and New Haven merchants traded with the West Indies.
With Boston the second largest distribution center in the entire
British Empire, Massachusetts had grown rich in trade. Her

two hundred and fifty thousand people stood first in political and cultural influence among all the North American colonies.

As Massachusetts had prospered, so too had her offshoot colonies. New Hampshire by 1763 had a population of fifty thousand, almost all of whom were engaged in very profitable forestry. Rhode Islanders now numbered about fifty-five thousand and had gained fame as accomplished smugglers, whose ships easily eluded British revenue cutters attempting to enforce customs regulations. Connecticut, whose population had swollen to more than two hundred thousand, grew rich by farming and feeding the seaport towns of New England.

Such were the thirteen colonies in 1763: waxing rich and strong after harsh beginnings, apparently as diverse from each other as they were from the mother country, but bound all together by allegiance to the world's greatest empire. As for any faint stirrings of disloyalty or hankerings after independence, Philadelphian Benjamin Franklin, who probably knew more about colonial opinion than any other man, would later declare of this era that he "never had heard in any Conversation from any Person, drunk or sober, the least Expression of a wish for a Separation, or Hint that such a Thing would be advantageous to America."

## THE WAY IT WAS:
### The Song of the Elders

"And when the Long Knives [Virginians] came to these shores we took them by the hand, and bid them welcome to sit down by our side, and live with us as brothers; but how did they requite our kindness? They at first asked only for a little land on which to raise bread for themselves and their families, and pasture for their cattle, which we freely gave them. They soon wanted more, which we also gave them. They saw the game in the woods, which the Great Spirit had given us for our substance, and they wanted that too. They penetrated into the woods in quest of game; they discovered spots of land which pleased them; that land they also wanted, and because we were loath to part with it, as we saw they had already more than they needed, they took it from us by force, and drove us to a great distance from our ancient homes.

"By and by the Dutchemaan arrived at Manahachta-nienk [Manhattan]. They wanted only a little, little land, on which to raise greens for their soup, just as much as a bullock's hide would cover. Here we might first have observed their deceitful spirit. The bullock's hide was cut up into little strips, and did not cover, indeed, but encircled a very large piece of land which we foolishly granted to them. They were to raise greens on it, instead of which they planted great guns; afterwards they built strong houses, made themselves masters of the island, then went up the river to our enemies, the Iroquois, made a league with them, persuaded us by their wicked arts to lay down our arms, and at last drove us entirely out of the country.

"When the Yengeese [English—a Mohican pronunciation which gave birth to the word Yankee] arrived at Machtitschwanne [Massachusetts], they looked about everywhere for good spots of land, and when they found one, they immediately and without ceremony possessed themselves of it; we were astonished, but still we let them go on, not thinking it worthwhile to contend for a little land. But at last when they came to our favorite spots, those which lay most convenient to our fisheries, then bloody war ensued: we would have been contented that the white people and we should have lived quietly side by side; but these white men encroached so fast upon us, that we saw at once we should lose all, if we did not resist them. The wars that we carried on against each other were long and cruel. We were enraged when we saw the white people put our friends and relatives, whom they had taken prisoner, on board of their ships, and carry them off to sea, whether to drown or sell them as slaves, in the country from which they came, we knew not, but certain it is that none of them have ever returned or even been heard of. At last they got possession of the whole of the country which the Great Spirit had given us. One of our tribes was forced to wander far beyond Quebec; others dispersed in small bodies, and sought places of refuge where they could; some came to Pennsylvania; others went far to the westward and mingled with other tribes. . . .

"We and our kindred tribes lived in peace and harmony with each other before the white people came into this country; our lands extended far to the north and far to the south. In the middle of it we would meet from all parts to smoke the pipe of peace together. When the white men arrived in the south we received them as friends; we did the same when they arrived in the east. It was we, it was our forefathers, who made them welcome, and let them sit down by our side. The land they settled on was ours. We knew not but the Great Spirit had sent them to us for some good purpose, and therefore we thought they must be a good people. We were mistaken; for no sooner had they obtained a footing on our lands than they began to seize them, first at one end and then at the other, and at last meeting each other in the center; where the council fire was yet burning bright, they put it out, and extinguished it with our own blood—with the blood of those who had received them, who had welcomed them in our land. Their blood ran in streams into our fire, and extinguished it so entirely, that not one spark was left us whereby to kindle a new fire; we were compelled to withdraw ourselves beyond the great swamp [the glades of the Allegheny Mountains] and to fly to our good uncles, the Delamattenos [Hurons] who kindly gave us a tract of land to live on. How long we shall be permitted to remain in this asylum, the Great Spirit only knows. The whites will not rest contented until they shall have destroyed the last of us, and made us disappear entirely from the face of the earth.

"I admit that there are good white men, but they bear no proportion to the bad; the bad must be the strongest, for they rule. They do what they please. They enslave those who are not of their color, although created by the same Great Spirit who created them. They would make slaves of us if they could, but as they cannot do it, they kill us. There is no faith to be placed in their words. They are not like the Indians, who are only enemies while at war, and are friends in peace. They will say to an Indian 'My friend! my brother!' They will take him by the hand, and at the same time destroy him. Remember! that this day I have warned you to beware of such friends as these. I know the Long Knives; they are not to be trusted."

Related by elders of the Lenape
and Mohican tribes to
Reverend John Heckewelder
in 1768

# 3 | The Imperial Headache

*A great empire has been established for the sole purpose of raising up a nation of customers . . .* —Adam Smith

On the morning after the jubilant victory celebrations of 1763 the British government awoke to several new and vexatious problems which had arisen out of the late war. The first of these was what to do with the loot. The loot in question being that vast western domain between the Alleghenies and the Mississippi which had been wrested from the French. It was known to be rich in furs, soil, game, and—warlike Indians.

During the Seven Years' War many of the western tribes had fought on one side or the other; those who helped the English had been promised not only guns, rum, loot, and as many French scalps as they could tie to their belts, but also that henceforth their lands would be respected. Solemn promises had been made to various tribes, and this time (unlike all other times before or since) the Great White Father in London determined that his promises should be kept. His motives were not, however, humanitarian; they were economic.

First of all, warfare against the Indians cost money. When, in 1763, certain Ohio Valley tribes gathered together under the half-crazed leadership of one Pontiac and brought bloody devastation to the area around Pittsburgh, the uprising had to be put down by several battalions of Scots Highlanders —a costly business to which the colonies contributed not a farthing. Furthermore, Indian warfare disrupted the very valuable fur trade. But the western frontier would never know peace so long as colonial settlers kept encroaching on Indian lands and massacring His Majesty's red-skinned subjects in the process.

Secondly, there was the potentially explosive question of land claims. Various colonies claimed each other's western frontier regions, and land-speculation companies were sprouting like weeds in both America and England. Before absolute chaos ensued, the king's ministers prevailed upon him to issue an imperial decree. This Proclamation of 1763 was intended as a temporary stopgap measure which would "freeze" the frontier question until a workable policy could be thought out. It declared that until further notice no colonial government could grant, and no white man take, land beyond the crest of the Alleghenies. It all seemed perfectly reasonable in London.

But not in the colonies. There, to the distress and mortification of royal officials, western frontiersmen and settlers simply ignored the royal decree. Daniel Boone and his "Long Hunters" opened up the Kentucky region, and Virginians poured over the Blue Ridge. Pennsylvanians and New Yorkers, undeterred by the recent Pontiac Conspiracy, began flocking into the Ohio country. Nothing less than a large standing army, it seemed, could possibly stem the tide of colonial migration or enforce respect for the law. But Britain could not afford to maintain a large standing army in North America—only a few regiments, and those in the seaport towns.

These regiments were left behind at the end of the Seven Years' War, in order, some said, to provide employment for deserving British officers who would otherwise have to be retired on half pay. The citizens of Halifax, Philadelphia, New York, and other towns where these troops were quartered raised a howl of protest; it was un-English to quarter troops among civilians in peacetime. Un-English it might have been, but not unnecessary, as the regrettable affair of the Paxton uprising in Pennsylvania demonstrated.

A band of frontier hoodlums from around the settlement of Paxton in western Pennsylvania, furious over the lack of protection afforded them by the Philadelphia authorities during the Pontiac Conspiracy, took their bloody revenge by massacring the peaceful Conestoga Indians of Lancaster County. Having butchered the men, women, and children of this tribe, the "Paxton Boys" then set out to murder the equally innocent Moravian Christian Indians. These fled to Philadelphia, where they were protected by the regular British garrison. The "Boys," fifteen hundred strong, heavily armed, mostly drunk and with blood in their eyes, marched upon Philadelphia in 1764. In the end, Benjamin Franklin talked them all into going home (by promising bounties for "hostile" Indian scalps). Un-English or not, the city fathers thanked heaven for that British garrison.

But the problems of western lands and the quartering of troops in the colonies were not the only elements of the imperial hangover of 1763. Most of the headache was financial. It now cost Britain £350,000 a year to administer the colonies, and Great Britain's national debt at war's end stood at £130,000,000 (having doubled during the struggle). In order to pay for all this, Englishmen (especially landowners and businessmen) were to be heavily taxed. Americans were Englishmen too, so why shouldn't they too be taxed? And since the late war had largely been fought to protect and extend the North American colonies, it seemed doubly just that they should now shoulder their fair share of the costs. In fact, it was time, felt His Majesty's ministers, that the formerly haphazard relations between colonies and home country be placed upon some better regulated footing. But in setting out to accomplish this desirable end, the British ruling classes were, unfortunately for all involved, burdened by a Theory.

This theory, which we know as mercantilism, although uncodified, had become more and more explicit in western Europe ever since a money economy had replaced the barter of the Middle Ages. In its most primitive form, the mercantilist theory held that real wealth in this world consisted of money—gold, silver, perhaps precious gems. After all, the very security of the monarchy—and hence of the nation—depended finally upon the king's ability to pay his mercenary armies and fleets in the good, hard coin-of-the-realm that they demanded. As for raw materials, manufactured goods, and services—until these had been sold for real money, they represented only potential, not actual, wealth. Moreover, as everyone knew, there was only a limited amount of gold and silver in the world; therefore it behooved every national government to grab as much of this limited amount of real wealth for itself as it could.

Basically developed as the theory of a commercial (rather than an industrial) economy, mercantilist thought was firmly grounded upon one grand idea. This grand idea (which remains the philosophical guide of merchants and businessmen to the present day) was simply: Buy Cheap and Sell Dear. It was, of course, better to buy cheap with goods (which were not real money) and sell dear for gold or silver (which were). Best of all was not to buy, but simply to steal (from Orientals, Africans, or whoever else could be bullied) whatever could later be sold for cash. To ensure that all this was done as cheaply and efficiently as possible, trade and commerce would be strictly regulated by the government. The nation would be one large cartel, its ruling class the board of directors.

For a long time the role of overseas colonies in this happy scheme of profit-making was not well defined. Everyone could see the direct benefits of plundering the gold and silver of Mexico and Peru or the precious gems of India. And most people could perceive the slightly less direct profits to be made by stealing from the heathen such easily negotiable items as spices, furs, or black slaves—even if you had to pay for such commodities with glass beads or trinkets. But how best to turn a penny from vast wilderness colonies inhabited by one's own people? As the eighteenth century dawned, so did an answer to this problem. The overseas colonies could provide such raw materials as furs, opium, tobacco, rum, slaves, cotton, or what-have-you to the home country. These could then either be re-sold directly to foreigners or manufactured into salable arti-cles. The colonial raw materials would be paid for by exporting manufactured articles to the colonists (who would be forbidden to produce such things for themselves). In other words, barter within the empire—sell for cash outside it. True, a certain limited amount of real money would have to flow between the colonies and the home country, but this real money stayed within the family, so to speak—no nasty foreigners could get their paws on a penny of it.

Most of the benefits of such a system would accrue, of course, to the home country. But this was only just and proper. Who, after all, had established, financed, and nursed the col-onies in the first place? Who had defended them (at consider-able annoyance and expense) against foreign attack? Some disgruntled critics insisted that the benefits of the mercantilist system really accrued only to the home country's *ruling class* and not to the people. But they were easily answered. For it has always been the most cherished belief of the rich (and remains so today) that *their* prosperity ensures the well-being of everyone else, as wealth trickles down to the masses from on high.

Such, in brief outline, was the mercantilist view of the world. Those who held it made the history of three centuries seem like little more than a record of struggle between rival, heavily armed supermarket chains. Ironically, just as a stricter application of mercantilist laws began to bring disaster to Britain's new empire, the theory itself was being challenged and demolished by younger, more realistic political economists. But Adam Smith had not yet published his *Wealth of Nations* —and if he had, it is certain that none of the ministers of George III would have either read or understood it.

Britain's means of regulating trade within the empire were three: Acts of Trade and Navigation, Orders in Council, and, of course, customs taxes. Both Acts of Trade and Naviga-tion and customs taxes had to be adopted by Parliament.

Orders in Council were issued by the king's ministers, generally upon the advice of Admiralty lords. All of these methods of establishing and securing mercantilist benefits were venerable. They had been used since the time of the early Tudor kings without much objection from any of His Majesty's colonial subjects. But the reason for that was simply that Acts of Trade and Navigation, insofar at least as they applied to the North American colonies, had not been very strictly enforced. Colonials were in the habit of complying with those acts they deemed beneficial to themselves and simply ignoring the others. British ministers, although well aware of the situation, had generally followed former Prime Minister Robert Walpole's policy of treating the colonies with "a salutary neglect." When they did not, they were liable to receive unpleasant surprises.

Take, for example, the matter of writs of assistance. In 1760, while waging a world war against France and Spain, British Prime Minister William Pitt very understandably found it intolerable that British subjects in North America should carry on a large and totally illegal molasses trade with the French and Spanish West Indian islands. Not only did this trade profit His Majesty's enemies in time of war; it also denied the British treasury badly needed revenue with which to prosecute that war. In order to put an end to this treasonable and injurious activity, Pitt ordered that the Sugar Act of 1733 (which placed a prohibitively high customs tax upon molasses imported into the colonies from sources outside the empire) be rigidly enforced. Royal customs collectors in North American ports such as Boston, New York, and Charleston were instructed to search out and tax or seize all the smuggled molasses hidden in merchants' warehouses. But of course they were to do this in a strictly legal manner. So customs collectors began applying to superior colonial courts for writs of assistance. These were general search warrants empowering an officer of the crown to enter any premises in search of smuggled goods.

All of this seemed so eminently just and reasonable that British ministers were stunned by the violence of colonial reaction. Speeches were made and pamphlets issued against the "tyrannical writs"; customs collectors were threatened by mobs—some were beaten. Since colonial agitators could not come right out in defense of smuggling or trading with the enemy, they attacked the legality of the writs themselves. Lawyer James Otis, representing a group of Massachusetts merchants, went to court in Boston to have the writs withdrawn. He argued that since the writs were general rather than specific search warrants, they endangered the rights of freeborn Englishmen. In the courtroom "Otis was a flame of fire," observed spectator John Adams. "Every man of an immense crowded audience appeared . . . to go away, as I did, ready to take arms against writs of Assistance." In the end, few customs collectors (long accustomed as they were to being bribed by colonial merchant-smugglers) cared to enforce the Sugar Act. The Seven Years' War came to its victorious conclusion, Pitt resigned from the ministry, and "salutary neglect" once again prevailed.

But not for long. As we have seen, Britain's prolonged struggle against France and Spain had proven ruinously expensive. English landowners and rich businessmen who sat in Parliament (or owned the men who sat there) were determined that colonials must share the costs of empire. Therefore, in March 1764, the new chancellor of the exchequer (secretary of the treasury), George Grenville, introduced a measure in Parliament known as the Revenue Act. This law raised the import duties to be paid by colonials for sugar, wine, coffee, silk, and linen. At the same time, Grenville's Revenue Act lowered the tax on imported molasses so as to do away with smuggling. After all, reasoned Grenville, if colonial merchants were willing to bribe customs officials sixpence per gallon to *avoid* the tax, perhaps they'd be willing to *pay* the tax if it was reduced to only threepence per gallon. And to encourage still more honesty, Grenville saw to it that jurisdiction over cases involving customs taxes was now transferred from colonial courts (where juries seldom convicted smugglers) to Admiralty courts. There, unhampered by juries, a board of naval officers would pass judgment.

Once again, these seemingly reasonable measures raised a storm of protest in the colonies. The New York assembly declared that "exemption from the burthen of ungranted, involuntary taxes, must be the grand principle of every free state." And a continent-wide boycott against all the articles listed in the Revenue Act of 1764 was organized; rather than pay import taxes on these articles, colonials would do without them.

But colonial discontent over the Revenue Act of 1764 was mild compared to the storm which greeted Grenville's next plausible attempt to raise money in North America, the Stamp Act of 1765. This was the first direct internal tax ever to be levied in the colonies, and its burden was aggravated by its nuisance value. It applied to every kind and description of legal document. College or school diplomas, liquor or other licenses, appointments to office, every copy (not merely every issue) of newspapers or almanacs, and a multitude of other documents were covered. They would now have to be printed upon specially embossed paper (the purchase of which from official distributors constituted payment of the tax) or brought to a stamp office where an official would emboss them.

Stamp taxes had long been in use in England (they are still in use in most Latin countries), and Parliament saw nothing unusual in extending them to the colonies. Debate over the matter in the House of Commons was minimal, aside from a brief exchange between Charles Townshend (one of the "king's friends" clique) and Colonel Isaac Barré (an old comrade-in-arms of General Wolfe). When Barré questioned the new measure, Townshend irritatedly demanded to know whether "these American children, planted by our care, nourished by our indulgence . . . and protected by our arms," would be so ungrateful as to refuse their small share of imperial revenues. Barré took exception. Praising the colonials as "Sons of Liberty," he replied: "*They* planted by *your* care? No, your oppression planted them in America. . . . *They* nourished up by *your* indulgence? They grew by your neglect of them. . . . *They* protected by *your* arms? They have nobly taken up arms in your defence . . ."

Of course, the new stamp taxes fell most heavily upon lawyers, merchants, and publishers—the very people who were most articulate in the colonies. They hastened to organize resistance. They did this by persuading workers in the port cities that stamp taxes would cripple business and thus lead to widespread unemployment. The workers thereupon formed groups called (after Barré) Sons of Liberty. In cities and towns throughout North America the Sons of Liberty began to enforce a stricter boycott of English goods. Henceforth no goods at all would be imported from Great Britain. Backed by the Sons of Liberty, upper-class orators and agitators were able to arouse the poor. From Boston to New York, from Philadelphia to Charleston, they harangued the "rabble," warning that this "loathsome" stamp tax (which had no impact at all upon the poor) would not only lead to unemployment and poverty, but was a conspiracy of British politicians to "enslave" all colonials. Soon violent mobs were roaming the streets of the principal colonial cities. In Boston such a mob destroyed the house of Royal Lieutenant Governor Thomas Hutchinson. In New York customhouses were sacked. In Philadelphia royal officials were made to swear they would never sell any of the "accursed" stamps. In Charleston mobs threatened to tar and feather any and all tax collectors. Meantime, the merchant and lawyer patrons of the Sons of Liberty organized a "congress" of representatives from nine of the colonies, which met in New York in the fall of 1765. This "Stamp Act Congress" had the temerity to declare that Parliament had no right at all to levy taxes in the colonies!

But it was the American boycott of English goods that really hurt. Before the end of 1765, Americans had canceled more than £700,000 in orders. Worse than that, they were threatening not to pay the more than £4,000,000 they owed to British merchants. As the months passed, British manufacturers who depended heavily upon the colonial trade began to face bankruptcy, and unemployed British workers muttered threateningly in the streets. Parliament was flooded by petitions for relief. Bowing to the pleas of British businessmen, Parliament finally repealed the Stamp Act in March 1766. They simultaneously passed a Declaratory Act, which asserted that Parliament had the right to "make laws and statutes . . . to bind the colonies in all cases whatsoever." But British politicians began to wonder if they would ever be able to collect taxes in America, or if they even dared to try. When, in 1767, Charles Townshend succeeded Grenville as chancellor of the exchequer, Grenville taunted him about it in Parliament: "You are cowards, you are afraid of the Americans, you dare not tax America!" Townshend (slightly drunk at the time) replied: "Fear? Cowards? Dare not tax America? *I* dare tax America!" "Dare you tax America?" Grenville sneered. "I wish to God I could see it!" "I will, I will!" Townshend shouted. And he did.

Since the colonial upper classes had raised such a rumpus over direct internal taxation, claiming it to be in violation of their charters, Townshend decided to revert to the old, tried-and-true method of taxing colonial imports and exports. This was a matter of regulating imperial trade—something no one (not even the most radical of colonial lawyers) had ever suggested Parliament had not the right to do. The Townshend Acts, passed in 1767, levied import duties on such English manufactures entering America as glass, paint, paper, and the East India Company's tea. But at the same time such colonial exports as grain and whale oil were to be allowed to enter England tax-free and a bounty was even to be paid to American exporters of hemp, flax, and timber. On balance, the Townshend Acts seemed at least as favorable to colonial businessmen as to the British treasury. And, besides, customs revenues would go not only to the crown; they would also help pay for the very necessary defense of the colonies themselves and pay the salaries of royal governors and judges—thereby relieving colonial taxpayers of that burden. To ensure that all of this was handled honestly and impartially, a new American Board of Commissioners of Customs was established with head-quarters in Boston. This would do away with the bribery and corruption of customs collectors and help put an end to smuggling. What honest merchant could object to that?

As a matter of fact, many did not. There were, to be sure, outcries against all the new paperwork imposed by the Board of Commissioners—the usual businessman's complaint against government bureaucracy. But colonial merchants and lawyers found it harder to incite mobs against import duties than they had against the Stamp Act. Nor were so many merchants themselves persuaded that the Townshend duties would prove ruinous to their trade. When boycotts and non-importation agreements were once again organized against English trade, they were really effective only in New York and New England; trade between Great Britain and colonial ports south of New York actually increased during the next few years. But on the whole, though not so grievously as in the past, British trade with America did suffer after Charles Townshend accepted Grenville's dare—and British merchants again began complaining to Parliament.

But by this time George III and his parliamentary allies, the "king's friends," were getting a firm grip upon the British government. The enforcement of the Townshend Acts coincided, roughly, with that civil strife in London which culminated in the Massacre of St. George's Fields. The use of armed force struck terror into the hearts of many of the king's opponents; bribery bought others; the fear of bloody civil war silenced the rest. An American observer, Josiah Quincy, wrote in 1769: "Never did the people engage in the struggle for liberty under so many disadvantages. . . . Never was public virtue at so low an ebb nor ministerial influence (by means of places, pensions, etc.) so unlimited. Never were the people so unarmed, so unskilled, so unprepared to exert force, nor the Administration so well furnished with every means of subverting the constitution." Having perfected his political machine, the king had found ministers with whom he could work.

Foremost among these was Lord Frederick North, who in 1770 combined the jobs of First Lord of the Treasury, party boss in the House of Commons, and prime minister. He was a fat, hearty, good-natured man with few ambitions, who worked hard and hoped that everything would come out all right in the end—somehow. Personally honest, he was quite willing to dole out bribes in order to manage the king's corrupt party machine. Argument and abuse simply rolled off his impervious hide; he would placidly doze in the House of Commons while opponents shouted at him. He believed absolutely in the benevolence of his king, the roast beef of Olde England, and keeping things as they were. He was, in fact, the original prototype of Colonel Blimp.

Lord Chief Justice and political whip in the House of Lords for the "king's friends" clique was William Murray, Baron Mansfield. A crusty, frosty lawyer, Mansfield had devoted his entire adult life to feathering his own nest. He had a magnificent contempt for the law and once advised a fellow barrister: "If you have no case, attack the plaintiff's lawyer." The people of London expressed their opinion of Mansfield by mobbing his coach in the streets and burning his house in Bloomsbury Square. He was especially detested in the colonies, where he was looked upon as a particularly malevolent enemy of colonial rights. Indifferent to criticism, he once remarked of the colonial legislatures: "Madness is catching in all popular assemblies."

Commanding Britain's chief weapon, her fleet, was the Earl of Sandwich, First Lord of the Admiralty. Aside from devising a new use for two slices of bread and allowing the Royal Navy to rot in harbor, the earl was chiefly famous for his personal wickedness. When he once taunted the popular hero, John Wilkes, that he would surely die either upon the gallows or of venereal disease, Wilkes replied: "That depends, My Lord, on whether I embrace your principles or your mistress." Of Sandwich it might well be said (and was) that he was "Too infamous to have a friend, / Too bad for bad men to commend."

Another of the king's more notorious ministers was Lord George Germain, secretary of state for the colonies. Germain had been born George Sackville and had later (in order to receive a legacy) changed his name to Germain. He had received his early training serving with the British army in Ireland—that harsh school of imperial oppression. Later, disobedience to orders and personal cowardice led to his court-martial and dismissal in disgrace from the army. A supreme egotist, given to violent temper tantrums, he liked to compare himself to Spain's great colonial oppressor, the Duke of Alva—without, apparently, recalling that, for all Alva's victories, Spain eventually lost her Dutch provinces. Germain remained defiantly ignorant of conditions in North America, and to the end of his days would insist that all but a handful of perversely evil colonials were really loyal to Good King George.

And, finally, among the more prominent of the crown's ministers, was the secretary of state for war, William Shute, Viscount Barrington (successor to Lord Weymouth). His job—the recruitment and administration of the army, was vital to the king during these times of popular unrest. But Barrington's sole recommendation for his post seemed to be his uncanny skill as a politician—his ability to survive in office despite all disasters. An experienced and polished grafter, he once observed that "he could compare the state to a great plum pudding, which he was so fond of that he would never quarrel with it, but should be taking a slice as long as there was any left."

These were the men (and others of their ilk) who arose in the demoralized aftermath of the Seven Years' War to guide the destinies of the world's greatest empire through desperately trying and perilous times. It was almost as if the Watergate conspirators had been called upon by fate to govern the Union during the American Civil War.

In later years George III and Lord North were to be portrayed to generations of Americans as bloodthirsty monsters. But neither of them had any personal prejudice against Americans. On the contrary, both had supported the repeal of the Stamp Act, and in 1770, when North became chief minister (Charles Townshend had died a year earlier), he decided, with the king's full support, to make a conciliatory gesture to the colonies. He repealed the Townshend customs taxes—all of them except the one on tea. This tea tax didn't much matter, because colonials had long been used to smuggling in almost all the tea they drank. The king thought it ought to be retained simply "as a mark of the Supremacy of Parliament."

General rejoicing greeted the end of the Townshend Acts in the colonies. Boycotts and non-importation agreements ended, and, to the great satisfaction of sober businessmen on both sides of the Atlantic, British-American trade quickly resumed its normal, profitable course. As for the hated Board of Commissioners of Customs, on quiet instructions from London the commissioners relaxed their vigilance somewhat and eliminated much of that irritating bureaucratic red tape. The king and his ministers could now look forward to a period of calm on the colonial horizon.

And in England itself the political weather was also clearing. A bumper harvest in 1770 heralded the end of Britain's postwar economic slump. As prosperity began to return, the pressure of poverty was somewhat eased and even the poorest fell silent. "After a violent ferment in the nation," wrote Whig politician Edmund Burke in 1771, "as remarkable a deadness and vapidity has succeeded. . . . I do not suppose there is anything like this stupor in any period of our history."

THE WAY IT WAS:

*"A rage that knows no limits . . ."*

He was born into poverty on January 29, 1737, in the village of Thetford, a dreary hamlet about seventy miles northeast of London. His father spent an entire lifetime making ladies' corsets and barely avoiding debtors' prison. His mother, the daughter of an attorney, dreamed of better days long gone and "distressed" herself to send her only son to the village school. He was raised, as his mother wished, in the Church of England —but he inclined toward his father's denomination, the nonconformist Quakers. Years later he would be denounced as an enemy to all religion, but as a youth he was forced to study the Bible so thoroughly that he could quote long passages from memory to his dying day. His conscience was to be the stern, unforgiving voice of the Old Testament.

In school he learned to read and write, listened avidly to his teacher's tales of a former life at sea, conceived a desire to "see the western side of the Atlantic," and utterly failed in his chief task—learning Latin. A knowledge of Latin was the first step to a career in medicine, religion, or law—the only ladders a lower-class boy could climb into a middle-class profession. Later he would be glad he failed Latin, for the child's genius, he claimed, "is killed by the barren study of a dead language and the philosopher is lost in the linguist." But at the time, his failure brought his formal education to an end when he was thirteen. He was then apprenticed to his father to make corsets, and, of course, he ran away from home three years later.

Dreaming of adventure, he tried to sign aboard the privateer *Terrible,* largely because her master called himself Captain Death. But his father found him before the ship sailed and persuaded him to give corsetry another chance. He did. Then his mother's nagging reproaches and his father's kindly "moral remonstrances" proved too heavy. Within a few months he ran away again, and this time he got to sea—in the privateer *King of Prussia.*

Evidently a privateersman's life was not as romantic as he'd imagined; he never talked or wrote of his life as a sailor— we don't even know how long he remained at sea. But early in 1757 he surfaced in London, working at his old trade as a journeyman corset maker. A year later he moved to Dover, and a year after that to the town of Sandwich, where he set himself up as a master corset maker and married a lady's maid named

Mary Lambert. Respectability lasted only a few months. His corset shop sank into bankruptcy, and "embarrassed with debts, and goaded by duns, he was thus obliged to depart in the night" with his tools, his wife, and a few belongings. The couple moved on to Margate, and there, less than a year later, Mary died.

A total failure, he swallowed his pride and returned to Thetford, but not to corset making. Instead, he studied to pass the government examination for a job with the excise service. The excise was an internal tax imposed on alcoholic beverages, tobacco, and other items. Both the tax and its collectors were hated by the public; smuggling to avoid the excise was both a national pastime and a large-scale industry. Furthermore, after expenses had been deducted, the job paid little more than a shilling a day—a near-starvation wage. But the ex–corset maker applied himself, passed the examination, and, on August 8, 1764, at the age of twenty-seven, became the excise collector for the village of Alford, north of Thetford on the North Sea. Within a year he was accused of having falsified his accounts (through laziness rather than dishonesty), admitted the truth of the charge, and found himself dismissed from his post.

He wandered down to London, where, according to a friend, he was "reduced to extreme wretchedness." Living on the streets, "he was absolutely without food, without raiment, and without shelter." Somehow he talked the headmaster of a private school in London into giving him a job as a teacher of English—but at this he also failed. He tried, for a time, to be a preacher—but that venture also ended badly. Finally, in July 1767, he petitioned the government to restore him to his old job as a tax collector. His letter was full of humiliating scrapings: "I humbly beg . . . I humbly hope . . . I humbly presume . . . I will endeavour that my future conduct shall as much engage your honors' approbation as my former has merited your displeasure . . ." but it paid off; in 1768 he was appointed excise tax collector for the town of Lewes.

This time he sincerely tried to make a go of it. He worked

hard at his tax collecting, made a point of making friends with some of the more substantial citizens, married a respectable widow named Elizabeth Ollive, and tried to manage her grocery business. He joined a local debating society and soon became known for his skill with words and "headstrong opinions." When the excise collectors throughout England petitioned Parliament for an increase in their salaries in 1772, his reputation for argument earned him a place on their steering committee. He wrote a pamphlet entitled *The Case of the Officers of Excise,* and hurried to London to see to its printing and distribution. He remained in London, lobbying on behalf of the excisemen, and there made the acquaintance of the playwright Oliver Goldsmith and the American philosopher Benjamin Franklin. Meantime, Parliament turned down the excise collectors' petition—instead, it voted to increase George III's personal allowance £100,000 per year.

His mission a failure, he returned to Lewes to find himself again dismissed from the excise service—for having spent so much time away from his post. His wife's grocery business now entered into bankruptcy, and soon there were official notices posted in Lewes announcing the auction of all his "household furniture, stock in trade and other effects. . . . Also a horse, a tobacco and snuff mill, with all the utensils for cutting tobacco and grinding off snuff; and two unopened crates of cream-colored stone ware." His second marriage did not survive this fresh financial disaster. His wife, Elizabeth, demanded and won a legal separation, "she engaging to pay her husband thirty-five pounds; and he promising to claim no part of whatever goods she might gain in the future."

Years later a critic was to write of him that he "seems everywhere to be transported with rage—a rage that knows no limits, and hurries him along like an impetuous torrent. . . . Such fire and fury . . . indicate that some mortifying disappointment is rankling at heart . . ." Mortifying disappointment indeed! Now, at the age of thirty-seven, he could recall nothing but mortification and disappointment: two wrecked marriages, several ruined careers, poverty, humiliation—a lifetime of failure and frustration.

Yet, even then, there must have been something redeeming about him. For when he decided, in despair, that his only chance was to seek a new life in the New World and asked his acquaintance Benjamin Franklin to write him a letter of introduction, Franklin characterized him as "well recommended," "ingenious," and "worthy." But Benjamin Franklin saw deeper and more charitably into human nature than did other men. In any event, armed with the good doctor's recommendation, his wife's thirty-five pounds, and unjustified optimism, in late September 1774 Thomas Paine set sail for America.

# 4 | The Colonial Grievance

*The Revolution was effected before the war commenced. The Revolution was in the minds and hearts of the people. . . . This radical change in the principles, opinions, sentiments, and affections of the people, was the real American Revolution.*

–John Adams

On the very day (March 5, 1770) that Parliament, trying to appease colonial sentiment, repealed the irksome Townshend Acts, a bloody brawl took place in Boston between English soldiers and a crowd of local toughs. It had nothing to do with customs duties or stamp taxes or boycotts or western lands; it had to do with labor trouble and reckless propaganda.

Trouble had been brewing ever since 1768. In that year the Commissioners of Customs had prosecuted a local Boston merchant named John Hancock for smuggling. Claiming that Hancock was being "framed," the Boston Sons of Liberty organized a mob to rescue Hancock and his sloop *Liberty*. Having accomplished this, the mob went on to rough up the commissioners, who fled to a fort in Boston Harbor. Royal Governor Sir Francis Bernard asked for protection, and it arrived—in the form of two regiments of British infantry sent down from Halifax. The troubles were resolved peacefully, but the regiments remained.

Like all soldiers far from home, the English troops in Boston wanted nothing better than to be friendly with the local populace—but they were given a very hard time. Local Boston self-styled "patriots" (those who opposed British economic regulations) got out a weekly scandal sheet known as the *Jour-*

*nal of Public Occurrences,* and in it, with depressing regularity, they cooked up perfectly false stories of drunken orgies, rapes, robberies, and other outrages supposedly committed by the soldiers upon the peaceful, law-abiding, respectable citizens of Massachusetts. When English troops went out into the town for a stroll, they were followed by gangs of children shouting "lobsterbacks!" at them. Any Bostonians who tried to be friendly were threatened by the "patriots" with a dose of tar and feathers. Individual soldiers were ambushed and beaten up by waterside roughnecks. Although the troops maintained admirable discipline in the face of these provocations, resentment mounted.

In February 1770 a few of the soldiers, to eke out their meager pay, took part-time jobs in a rope factory where the regular workers had gone out on strike. That led to a riot between the strikers and the strike-breaking soldiers in which a civilian was killed. Then, on the evening of March 5, a group of waterfront toughs ("Irish teagues and outlandish jack-tars," John Adams called them) led by an unemployed black sailor named Crispus Attucks began tossing rock-filled "snowballs" at a soldier standing guard at the customhouse on King (now State) Street. Twenty men of the main guard were called out and, with fixed bayonets, confronted the yelling mob of several hundred men and boys. After being taunted and stoned for more than half an hour, one soldier, who had been hit by a club, broke discipline and fired without orders into the crowd. Other soldiers began firing, and when the smoke had cleared, three men, including Crispus Attucks, lay dead and two more were mortally wounded.

The Boston "patriots" rubbed their hands together with ghoulish glee. This was just the kind of incident they'd been hoping for. They named the affair the "Boston Massacre" and sent pamphlets throughout the colonies describing it as a wanton murder of peaceable citizens by the brutal redcoats. Cries of outrage echoed back. But not all Bostonians were completely lost to decency. The English redcoats involved were defended at their trial by John Adams—and acquitted of murder. By that time the news of the repeal of the Townshend Acts had soothed American tempers—and a wave of prosperity soon quenched the uproar.

As one looks back today upon this "Boston Massacre," certain aspects of the affair seem remarkably up to date. There was a skillful use of reckless propaganda to whip up popular antagonisms (through such scandal sheets as the *Journal of Public Occurrences*). There was an organized threat of violence (through the Boston mob which roamed the streets shouting ugly slogans) to intimidate and muzzle the saner elements of the population. There was the swift seizure upon a local bread-and-butter issue (the ropemakers' strike), which converted a theoretical into a practical grievance. And, finally, there was a staged confrontation at which violence was deliberately provoked. Once the violence had occurred, the agitators had a new, ready-made "cause" to howl about. And behind the whole operation we can discern the workings of the "subversive" organization known as the Sons of Liberty. These tactics, first invented in America, were to be used successfully later by French Jacobins, Russian Bolsheviks, American Weathermen, and, most recently, by the Provisional Wing of the Irish Republican Army. They have become classical. Without the benefit of two centuries of hindsight, very few people in 1770 understood the workings of an underground movement. But to us it all seems painfully familiar.

Which brings us to the crux of the matter. No underground movement can operate in a vacuum; there has to be some basis of popular support, some widespread discontent or apprehension with which to work. In other words: Why did large numbers of Americans, wittingly or unwittingly, lend their support to a handful of malcontents and agitators?

Was it because of taxes? But direct taxes such as those on land or inheritances were nonexistent in several colonies and, where they did exist, were only one-twentieth of what Englishmen at home paid. Furthermore, the vast majority of colonials were too poor to pay any taxes at all and the wealthier minority very clever at avoiding them. Then what about customs taxes? Did these raise the price of imported manufactured goods to such an extent as to be a real burden? Well, as we have seen, very few items were so taxed, and then only intermittently. Furthermore, the cost of domestically manufactured items was very often as high as or higher than competitive imports. And where this was not the case (as, for example, with tea), import duties were widely avoided through smuggling—one of the colonies' largest industries.

Was it because of British regulation of colonial trade—the whole irritating machinery of the mercantilist system? It is certainly true that some shippers, merchants, and financiers felt the Acts of Trade and Navigation to be an intolerable barrier to "free enterprise." But if those acts imposed restrictions upon some colonial businessmen, they protected others. If the colonies were a captive market for British manufactured goods, England was a captive market for American raw materials. And, aside from subsistence farming, the export of such raw materials as lumber, tobacco, rice, and wheat was certainly the foundation of the colonial economy. Besides, Parliament's Acts of Trade and Navigation, like customs taxes, were continuously circumvented (where this was profitable) by smuggling. The remarkable fact was that even in that era of very vocal protest and dissent, at no time before 1775 did any significant number of colonials ever question the right of Parliament to regulate their trade either within or without the empire.

If they were not seriously troubled about taxes and trade regulations, perhaps the colonial masses were outraged by the Proclamation of 1763 and the closing of the western frontier to new settlement? Colonial land speculators certainly howled about it; but very few Americans could afford to speculate in western lands. The vast majority of frontiersmen and settlers, as we have seen, simply ignored the proclamation. They continued to spill over the Allegheny barrier and seize Indian lands as if no such proclamation had ever been made. The western settlers had grievances all right—very bitter grievances. But these were directed against their own colonial "establishments" back east and not against His Majesty's government in London. From New Hampshire to Georgia western settlers complained that their interests were ignored by eastern legislatures; that they received too little protection from Indian raids, that they were not represented in colonial capitals, that they had to travel hundreds of miles to find a court, that they could not afford legal fees, et cetera.

In the Carolinas these western grievances erupted into outright rebellion in 1769, when frontiersmen calling themselves "Regulators" organized to break up local courts, terrorize colonial officials, refuse to pay taxes or legal fees, and in general defy the silk-stockinged eastern gentry who ran the colony. On May 16, 1771, two thousand of these Regulators fought a pitched battle against colonial militia on the banks of Alamance Creek in North Carolina. The poorly armed Regulators lost, and most of them fled back to their piny woods. But fifteen of them were captured and six later hanged for treason —supposedly against the crown, but actually against the colonial establishment.

The American quarrel with England did not originate with rough frontiersmen or homespun settlers. It originated with the urban populations of the Atlantic seaboard cities. And when that quarrel finally erupted into war, most westerners either remained loyal to King George or kept out of the fighting.

If the masses of people in North America did not feel themselves intolerably oppressed by British taxes, trade regulations, or the all but unenforceable Proclamation of 1763, perhaps they were outraged by royal encroachments upon their political rights and liberties? Certainly in the years between 1763 and 1775 colonial "patriots" screamed their loudest—and most effectively—on this theme. There was no surer way for an orator to whip a crowd into a frenzy than by convincing them that their rights as freeborn Englishmen were being threatened. But what were the facts?

British subjects in North America, with the exception of the blacks, were the freest people in the world. They were freer, in fact, than Englishmen at home. While enjoying all the historic rights and privileges of Englishmen, they escaped certain English feudal hangovers. There were no tithes to support an established church. Wages were not regulated, nor were there any guilds to which workers had to belong. Americans were exempt from naval press-gangs, and military service in time of war was purely voluntary. The colonial penal codes were much milder than those in England, and, finally, although social classes did exist, they were neither rigid nor oppressive. As English visitor Janet Schaw observed, 'a most disgusting equality" prevailed.

As for their rights of self-government, Americans enjoyed more autonomy in 1770 than any colonial people had ever known before or were ever to know until the twentieth century. True, king and Parliament in England had undisputed control over foreign affairs, war and peace and imperial trade. But in almost all other respects Americans governed themselves. Colonial assemblies had exclusive rights to tax their own people, appoint officials of all kinds (and fix their salaries), commission military officers and raise troops as they chose, control their own schools and churches, organize their own land tenure laws, and establish and regulate their own judicial system (though final appeals could be carried to the Privy Council in London). There were, to be sure, royal governors in each colony who enjoyed a veto power over acts of the colonial assemblies, but that power was rarely exercised. Royal governors, whether native born or sent out from England, had to live, after all, with their colonial subjects. They were a very long way from parliamentary instructions, royal supervision, and military support. A royal governor of Massachusetts or South Carolina was likely to prove a far more agreeable and accommodating fellow in Boston or Charleston than he may have pretended to be in London.

On the whole, then, it would seem, from an objective viewpoint, that no matter how loudly certain colonial agitators may have howled, most of His Majesty's North American subjects had few reasonable grounds for complaint about their situation. But people do not always (or, indeed, very often) view matters objectively or act from reasoned motives. In attempting to find causes for great historic movements or events, it is most important to discover what the people involved *thought* they were doing. What, then, did the majority of Americans *think* they were doing in the decade before fighting broke out?

In 1842 a young lawyer named Mellen Chamberlain interviewed Captain John Preston, a ninety-one-year-old veteran of the battles at Concord and Lexington. "Did you take up arms against intolerable oppressions?" Chamberlain asked.

"Oppressions?" Preston responded. "I didn't feel them."

"What, were you not oppressed by the Stamp Act?"

"I never saw one of those stamps. I certainly never payed a penny for one of 'em."

"Well, what then about the tea tax?"

"I never drank a drop of that stuff; the boys threw it all overboard."

"Then I suppose you had been reading Harrington or Sidney and Locke about the eternal principles of liberty."

Never heard of 'em. We read only the Bible, the Catechism, Watts' Psalms and Hymns, and the Almanac."

"Well, then, what was the matter? And what did you mean in going to the fight?"

"Young man, what we meant in going for those red-coats was this; we always had governed ourselves, and we always meant to. They didn't mean that we should."

Which may stand as a very fair summation of what most colonials *thought* the argument was all about from 1763 to 1775. They were not really vexed by taxes or regulations or "oppressions"; neither were they attempting to gain their liberty—they already enjoyed that. Nor were they trying to win the right to self-government; as Captain Preston pointed out, they "always had" governed themselves. Rather, they conceived themselves to be *defending* their right to self-government against some real or imaginary threat of *coming* tyranny.

Well, how real or imaginary was this threat? Did George III and/or his ministers or Parliament intend to establish a political despotism over the colonies? English liberal politicians like Charles Fox, Edmund Burke, and the radical John Wilkes did accuse the "king's friends" clique of entertaining such a scheme. But such accusations were, to some extent at least, the normal political sniping of out-of-office opposition leaders. No objective evidence exists to indicate that George III or any of his ministers planned to erect a tyranny in the colonies. But they did intend to govern the colonies in stricter accordance with British law—and British economic needs. The clumsiness of their attempts to do this could easily be made to look (by clever propagandists) like steps in a sinister conspiracy. And of clever propagandists there was never any lack in the colonies.

Take, for example, Samuel Adams of Boston—ex–Harvard student, ex–Puritan minister, ex-lawyer, failed businessman, and expert politician. The family fortunes had been ruined by an act of Parliament which closed down his father's Massachusetts Land Bank. Turning to politics, young Sam joined the Boston Caucus Club and held a variety of minor offices in the city administration; he was elected to the Boston assembly in 1765. His principal weapon was his pen (he was not a very skillful orator), which he wielded continuously. From 1748 to 1776 his articles and essays spread like a fever rash over the pages of such local newspapers as the *Independent Advertiser* and the *Boston Gazette*. So prolific was he that it has been estimated that Sam Adams wrote under at least twenty-five different names besides his own. His background fitted him perfectly for his task; he combined the moral zeal of the Puritan, the legal astuteness of the lawyer, the personal experience of the businessman, and the "inside" information of the politician. "I will oppose this tyranny at the threshold," he roared, "though the fabric of liberty fall, and I perish in its ruins." He was especially adept at manipulating working-class leaders in the Sons of Liberty organization—and, through them, the Boston mob.

Then there was Sam's cousin, John Adams—younger, with a better legal mind, much cooler, much more conservative, possessed of a very clear understanding of upper-class colonial interests. While Sam Adams's pen appealed to readers' emotions, John's remained sober and dignified. His writings were directed primarily to the recruitment of upper-class opinion "without" as he said, "all painting, pathos, rhetoric, or flourish of any kind." John Adams's legal niceties, and his ability to generalize particular grievances (he saw the Stamp Act as part of the history of tyranny beginning with ancient Egypt), perfectly supplemented his cousin's more flamboyant appeals.

Not much of a writer, but a brilliant orator, was Patrick Henry of Virginia. A member of the Virginia House of Burgesses from a backwoods county, Henry first achieved prominence in 1763, when the English Privy Council vetoed a measure he favored for regulating parsons' salaries. The king, Henry declared, "by annulling or disallowing Acts of so salutary a nature, from being the Father of his people degenerates into a Tyrant, and forfeits all rights to his subjects' obedience." While the assembled burgesses muttered nervously about "treason," Henry went on to lash the clergy (mostly Anglican) as "rapacious harpies who would . . . snatch from the hearth of their honest parishioner his last hoe-cake, from the widow and her orphan children their last milch cow!" Hardly an appeal to reason—but indicative of Henry's eloquence. Of course, Henry's audience was not really the silk-stockinged burgesses of tidewater Virginia—it was his own constituency, the aggrieved western settlers of the piedmont, to whom he was speaking.

Not that all upper-class Virginians were loyal to the crown. Aristocratic planters like George Washington, the Lee brothers, and Thomas Jefferson had many complaints against

British authority which regulated the export of their tobacco (sometimes at ruinously low prices) and kept them from lucrative speculation in western lands. Besides, they and their fellow plantation owners were in debt to English merchants to the tune of some £2,000,000. "Planters," Jefferson bitterly observed, "were a species of property, annexed to certain mercantile houses of London." Jefferson, a lawyer, was a budding politician; Washington was not. But one must never underestimate the influence of the opinions of substantial citizens like Washington, expressed in letters and private conversations rather than in public speeches or newspaper articles.

And there were others. There were James Otis ("like a flame"), Josiah Quincy ("Is not the bread taken out of your children's mouths and given unto the Dogs?" he roared), and Joseph Warren ("Your feet slide on the stones bespattered with your fathers' brains!" he screamed on the annual celebration of Boston Massacre Day)—all of Massachusetts. There were William Livingston of New York, who perceived that "clamour is at present our best policy," and John Dickinson, the deceptively mild Quaker from Pennsylvania, whose "Letters from an American Farmer" helped to stir up opposition to the Townshend Acts.

Nor should we forget the merchants for whom these lawyers spoke—men like John Hancock of Boston, who helped to finance the printing of pamphlets and who paid for the rum distributed to mobs of the faithful, or successful artisans like Paul Revere, who provided a much needed link with that important class of skilled urban craftsmen known in those days as "mechanicks." These last complained that "a colonial cannot make a button, a horseshoe, nor a hobnail, but some sooty ironmonger or respectable button maker of Britain shall bawl and squall that his honor's worship is most egregiously maltreated, injured, cheated and robbed by the rascally American . . ."

Note that almost all the leading colonial propagandists and agitators were members of the colonial "establishment."

They were educated, relatively wealthy individuals who, in most cases, had something personal to lose through continued British domination. Does this mean that their motives were entirely selfish? Does it mean that when Washington spoke of liberty, he really meant his own liberty from debt to British merchants? Does it mean that when John Adams spoke of independence, he really meant the independence of his wealthy merchant-clients from customs taxes? Was the entire "patriot" movement an exercise in hypocrisy?

No. Men tend to see the world from their personal perspective—and to generalize their personal experience and needs into universal truth. Having done so, they very often forget the personal or selfish motives which originally inspired their generalizations. And sometimes those generalizations correspond very well with a reality which is not yet perceived by their fellows. This was the case with the American colonial "patriots." We need not question their sincerity. They felt themselves aggrieved and were truly convinced that all Americans would share that grievance once matters were made clear to them.

But the "patriots," despite their influence and skill, could never have succeeded as individual voices in the wilderness. What they needed was an organization, and, as we have seen, they created one in the Sons of Liberty. This underground movement, though composed for the most part of city workers and the urban poor, was indirectly manipulated by the "establishment" malcontents. As time passed, the organization would change its form and often its name. It would be known locally as the Committee of Correspondence or the Committee of Public Safety or the Association—but its membership seldom varied and its over-all aim never. Its means were rough—but so was the age.

It was the Sons of Liberty who beat up royal officials, marched through the streets, burned opponents in effigy, tarred and feathered adversaries, and, in general, provided that element of terror and uproar which always cows the majority of any population. It was the violence provided by the Sons of Liberty groups that defeated the Stamp Act. Later (though by then the name of the organization had been changed in some colonies), the boycotts and non-importation agreements which defeated the Townshend Acts were "enforced" by these same groups. From the letters exchanged between leaders of the Sons of Liberty in various towns and cities emerged the Committees of Correspondence, which kept discontent alive between riots. Many years later John Adams would describe the organization as "that wonderful engine" of revolution.

Sam Adams was a virtuoso at manipulating this wonderful engine—he was, in fact, the only genuine *revolutionary* among colonial leaders, a man in the pattern of Robespierre or Trotsky. Well educated and coldly logical himself, he knew that most people are moved by emotion rather than reason, preferred drama to argument. Adams provided what they wanted—the Liberty Trees, the Phrygian liberty caps (which foreshadowed a later era's armbands), the rousing songs, the street demonstrations, and, always, plenty of rum. Such things, . he observed, "render the people fond of their leaders in the cause, and averse and bitter against all opponents."

But by 1771, with the Townshend duties repealed (except for the unimportant tax on tea) and the Boston Massacre a memory (which Adams kept alive and inflamed by annual observances), subversive activity subsided in the colonies. After all, the king and his ministers had backed down and, more important, prosperity had returned. John Hancock told the royal governor of Massachusetts that he was through with agitation. Benjamin Franklin (writing from London) advised his countrymen to quiet down. In New York, British soldiers were actually making friends among the populace. Virginia, wrote Thomas Jefferson, "seemed to fall into a state of insensibility." John Adams confided to his diary: "I shall certainly become more retired and cautious." And Sam Adams confessed: "Every day strengthens our opponents and weakens us."

What to do about it? Well, for one thing, Sam Adams picked a quarrel with Royal Governor Thomas Hutchinson of Massachusetts, a native-born, scholarly, not unkindly New Englander. When the Massachusetts assembly voted the governor his annual salary, Hutchinson refused it. He had already been paid, he said, by the king. This, of course, had been one of the reasons Parliament had taxed colonial business in the first place—to provide money for the payment of royal governors and royal judges in the colonies. It might be thought that colonial assemblies would welcome this measure as relieving them of a financial burden, but they bitterly opposed it. Their power over official salaries was, they felt, the power to control (to a certain extent) royal appointees. This was something for Adams to chew upon. He started a newspaper debate with Hutchinson about colonial rights—a debate which the governor was bound to lose against Adams's classical learning and fiery pen. But of greater importance, the debate enabled Adams to keep a flame of discontent alive among his followers, the "patriots."

Soon afterward the "patriots" had another and more explosive issue—the *Gaspée* affair. The *Gaspée* was a Royal Navy revenue cutter engaged in chasing smugglers in Narragansett Bay. While chasing one such smuggler, she ran aground on a sandspit below Providence. That night (June 10, 1772) a gang of local Sons of Liberty boarded her, beat up her captain and crew, and burned the ship. Very naturally, this attack upon a British naval vessel led royal officials to make an intensive search for the culprits, who would, of course, be sent to England for trial. Although none of the guilty could be found, this reminder that for certain crimes colonials could be tried in English courts provided new fuel for Sam Adams's "wonderful engine." Agitprop pamphlets and articles soon appeared screaming about "worse than Egyptian tyranny," "courts of inquisition," et cetera. It was certainly true that no principle of English liberty was more sacred than a man's right to be tried in his own community. The reminder that American traitors might legally be tried in England seemed to put a noose around every "patriot's" neck. But, in the upshot, no one was sent to England, no one was hanged. The "patriots" were, once again, at loose ends.

Of course, there were always "standing" grievances, so to speak, which might be exploited. But these were mainly in the unexciting realms of theory. One of the most venerable and well known of these (and one about which generations of later Americans were to hear overmuch) was summed up in the colonial slogan "No Taxation without Representation!" Since this phrase has acquired such a revered place in the pantheon of American "fighting words," it might be useful to examine it more closely.

What colonials meant by the slogan was simply that since they were not represented in Parliament, the British government had no right to tax them at all. It was an ancient "right" of Englishmen not to be taxed without their consent—that is to say, without the consent of their representatives. But this right was theoretical, not practical. After all, as we have seen, the great majority of Englishmen could not vote and so were, strictly speaking, unrepresented in Parliament—yet no one questioned Parliament's right to tax everyone at home. Americans today who do not vote, or who vote for losing candidates, might raise the same slogan and refuse to pay taxes levied by Congress because they are not, strictly speaking, represented in that body. But they do not. The reason they do not is that members of Congress, like members of Parliament, are assumed to represent *all* the people of their districts, no matter how many of those people voted for them. This is known as "virtual" representation, and was so known to Englishmen on both sides of the Atlantic in colonial times.

But there were no members of Parliament "virtually" representing anyone in America, since there were no election districts in America, nor, with the means of communication available in the eighteenth century, could there have been. So it would seem that the colonials were right to protest. But, aside from the abortive stamp tax, the British government *never* did attempt to collect direct internal taxes (though they did claim the *right* to do so). As for external customs taxes, these were used, supposedly, only to regulate trade. As long as they wanted to stay in the empire (which, until 1776, the overwhelming majority of colonials did), Americans could hardly claim that Parliament had no right to regulate imperial trade. Colonial agitators tried to make an issue of the fact that the Grenville and Townshend Acts were intended not only to regulate trade but to raise money through indirect taxation. But here they began splitting hairs and generally lost the interest of their colonial audiences.

And so, by 1773, the colonial grievance machine was barely sputtering along for lack of fuel. But genial, simpleminded Lord North and his hard-working, dull, dutiful master, George III, were about to provide a whole tankful of explosives.

## THE WAY IT WAS:

### Tribulations of a Farmer

In December 1758 a veteran of the late French and Indian wars on the western frontiers retired in disgust from the army. The last campaign had been a deep humiliation. Although he considered himself something of an expert on military affairs, and had read all the proper classical treatises on the subject, his superior officers consistently ignored his advice. And when he demanded that they distinguish him "from the *common run* of provincial officers," they simply smirked at his presumption. The orders he received were, he complained, "dark, doubtful and uncertain; today approved, tomorrow condemned." Although often insubordinate himself, he demanded the strictest obedience from the men he commanded. Two who broke discipline he had hanged from a gallows forty feet high as an "encouragement" to the rest. And finally, in the presence of the enemy, at the most critical moment of a decisive battle, he blunderingly led his troops into a firefight with their own comrades, in which fourteen of them perished. Perhaps, after all, the military life was not for him.

But there was always the farm, or "plantation," as the early settlers had called their cultivated lands. He had inherited this property (on the banks of the Potomac in tidewater Virginia) from his half brother and now, with his martial career at an end, he devoted himself to improving it. Like almost all the tidewater plantations, his was devoted to the production of tobacco and corn "without any dressing," he observed, "till the land is exhausted." Having once visited Barbados, he had noticed how the island planters had made use of manures to enrich their soil. He now copied them. Carefully reading all the latest recommended farm manuals, he became convinced that crop rotation was essential. Soon he was planting fallow fields with grass seed, experimenting with oats and barley, and, finally, devoting a large share of his acreage to wheat. He also built his own mill, established a textile industry (which, by 1768, was producing some two thousand yards of woolen, cotton, and linen cloth annually), started raising sheep instead of cattle, and even lowered nets into the Potomac to catch fish. All of which greatly amused his more conservative neighbors.

He himself rarely found anything amusing. Applying to farm management the mathematical outlook of a surveyor (which he had once been) and the discipline of a soldier, he ran his work force of black slaves and white indentured servants with strict efficiency. He made what were probably the first time-and-motion studies ever to be conducted in North America to be sure that he was getting the most from his laborers. If a slave sulked under this system, he immediately sold the "wretched creature" to one of the dreaded West Indian plantations. This did not, however, prevent him from condemning the slave trade—in theory.

As a planter he now found himself enmeshed in the complex network of mercantilist laws by which Britain regulated trade with her colonies. He could not sell his tobacco or wheat directly to a foreign country. He must transport his produce across the Atlantic only in British ships and only to British ports, even though two-thirds of it was usually destined for the Continent. Furthermore, he had to buy all his supplies, whether European or English, from British merchants.

In practice a planter consigned his yearly harvest to some British merchant for later sale. The merchant deducted freight, storage, insurance, warehousing, inspection, and unloading fees, as well as import taxes and his own commission from the proceeds of a sale before any cash was credited to the planter's account. During depression times these charges often exceeded the sale value of the planter's produce. In that case, the merchant would generally lend a planter money while holding a lien against next year's crops to secure the debt—and charge a healthy interest rate for the loan.

In the vessel carrying a planter's crops to England, he usually sent a written order for various manufactured goods which the merchant was to buy and ship to him out of the proceeds from the sale of his crop. For this service British merchants also charged. Furthermore, when suppliers found that their goods were destined for the colonies, they often supplied broken, worn-out, or shoddy articles.

The retired military-man-turned-planter ordered busts of Alexander the Great and Julius Caesar from London, as well as such items as nails ("mean in quality," he complained, "but not in price"), hoes, scythes ("some crooked and some straight"), fruit, tools, paper, playing cards, household utensils, and snuff. Goods arrived at his plantation broken; cloth was often moth-eaten. Some orders arrived months late, some not at all. "We have often articles sent us," he wrote to his London merchants, Cary & Company, "that could only have been used by our forefathers in the days of yore." Once, when he ordered a spinet piano from London, he "begged as a favor that Mr. Cary would bespeak this instrument as for himself or a friend, and not let it be known that it is intended for exportation." After a few years' experience as a planter, he wrote bitterly to a friend, "Certain it is that our whole substance does already in a manner flow to Great Britain."

But if plantation management proved increasingly vexatious, there might be real profits to be made in western land speculation. Like all veterans of the recent war, he had been promised a slice of frontier wilderness as a discharge bonus. Being a man of substance and foresight, he began buying up, at cheap rates, bonus rights from other, needy veterans. Then he found business partners and organized a land company, to exploit an area near the forks of the Ohio River. In 1770 he made a trip to the wilderness with some of his associates and surveyed 62,000 acres along the south bank of the Kanawha River.

He was aware, of course, that the royal Proclamation of 1763 had forbidden any further encroachment upon the Indian lands west of the Alleghenies. But, as he wrote at that time, "I can never look upon that proclamation in any other light (but this I say between ourselves) than as a temporary expedient to quiet the Minds of the Indians." Confident of success, he staked out a personal claim to more than thirty thousand acres of the choicest bottomlands, and by 1774 he was ready to offer leases to prospective settlers. But just as this land speculation promised a profit, news arrived from England that promised ruin.

It seemed that His Majesty's Privy Council, having weighed the matter for more than a decade, now confirmed the proclamation line of 1763; the continental interior was to be reserved to the Indians and the fur trade. Still, he did not abandon all hope. His land claims were just east of the proclamation line, where settlement was still legal. But, of course, it was going to be a difficult matter trying to sell land to settlers who would be living on the other side of a river from potentially dangerous Indians. As if to underscore this fact, the

Shawnee nation went on the warpath later in 1774—and fighting centered on the Kanawha. Then, on March 21, 1775, came the final blow: Virginia's royal governor, Lord Dunmore, decided that all claims made along the Kanawha River had been obtained fraudulently—and promptly canceled them.

This was the last straw. Humiliated in the British military service, his plantation in debt to British merchants, his western land speculation ruined by British decree, George Washington began rereading his military manuals and training his neighbors in the rudiments of martial drill. Whatever happened next, he wanted to be ready.

# 5 | "The Die Is Now Cast ..."

*From the east to the west, blew the trumpet to arms,*
*Thro' the land let the sound of it flee,*
*Let the far and the near—all united with a cheer,*
*In defence of our* Liberty Tree.

–Tom Paine

Colonial mobs might prance around their Liberty Trees; backwoods philosophers might rant about such abstractions as "natural rights" and "liberty"; colonial agitators might write letters to one another; but to His Majesty's ministers in London pounds, shillings, and pence came first. And so, during the winter of 1772–73, the chief business before Parliament was not American discontent; it was the ruinous financial condition of that most important branch of the imperial supermarket, the East India Company.

Since many ministers, aristocrats, and members of Parliament owned shares in that venerable corporation, this was quite understandable. Due to mismanagement, corruption, and overextension, "John Company" had been ailing for some time; now he tottered on the brink of bankruptcy. And if the company went under, it would drag so important a sector of the British economy with it that a nationwide depression might ensue. Government would have to rescue the corporation (just as, in our day, Congress has rescued various American corporate giants). After much acrimonious debate, Parliament decided that the way to do this was to give the East India Company what amounted to a complete monopoly of the lucrative American tea trade.

Americans drank a lot of tea—about £6,000,000 worth annually. But up till now the East India Company had been prohibited from selling them any. It had been felt that the company's absolute monopoly on the importation of tea into England gave it advantage and profit enough. Other merchants deserved a share of the pie by exporting the tea from England to the colonies. Unfortunately, by 1772 the pie had almost vanished. Colonial merchants found it cheaper to buy their tea from the Dutch and smuggle it directly into America, thereby avoiding various taxes, commissions, freight charges, and so on. By the East India Company Act of 1773, Parliament sought to straighten out the matter. Henceforth the company would be allowed to ship its tea directly to America and sell it there through its own agents, thereby eliminating the middleman's profits.

Furthermore, the company would be excused from paying any customs taxes whatsoever on its tea trade—except for the old Townshend tax collected in American ports of entry. With these advantages the company could easily undersell all competitors in the colonial market—it could even undersell the smugglers. Thus, Parliament congratulated itself, several problems had been solved with one legislative stroke. The company had been saved from bankruptcy; a blow had been dealt against illegal smugglers; revenues had been increased; and Americans would pay less for their favorite beverage—they would even pay less than their English cousins buying tea in London.

At first glance it would seem that even such sharp lawyers as Sam Adams and his cousin would have difficulty finding a threat to liberty in the "Tea Act" (as Americans dubbed it). But they were equal to the challenge. Soon the colonial press was filled with articles about the "illegal monopoly" granted to the great company. Was this not the first wedge of a sinister plot whereby the company would be given the same privileges in North America that it enjoyed in India? Were Americans soon to be reduced to slavery if they continued to drink this "pestilential herb" from "the cup infused with bane by North's insidious hand"? When the tea tax was retained after repeal of the other Townshend duties, Americans had, by and large, simply ignored it as unimportant—a parliamentary face-saving device which had little practical impact. Now, however, it was seen that this tea tax was a dire threat to all colonial rights and liberties.

From May 1773, when news of the East India Company Act reached America, to December, when the first ships bearing the "accursed tea" arrived at colonial ports, Adams, Henry, and other propagandists beat the drums ever more wildly. Messages flew back and forth between the various Committees of Correspondence; the Sons of Liberty in port cities made ready to repel the tax invasion. It is a high tribute to the skill of colonial agitators that they were able to whip up a vast mass hysteria over so unexciting an issue.

In Charleston the tea was unloaded, but locked up in a damp warehouse where it would soon rot. At Philadelphia and New York the captains of the tea ships were "persuaded" by grim Sons of Liberty to turn back without landing their cargoes. But the Boston cell, irritated because someone had recently accused them of being "better at resolving what to do than in doing what they resolved," decided to put on a better show. Gathering at Old South Meetinghouse, under the direction of Sam Adams, they sent a message to Royal Governor Hutchinson demanding that he order the three tea ships in harbor to return to England. When Hutchinson refused (he could not legally comply), Adams declared: "This meeting can do nothing further to save the country." On cue, a mob disguised as Mohawk Indians rushed down to the waterfront, boarded the tea ships, and emptied 342 big chests of the "pestilential herb" into the harbor. A large audience applauded their efforts. There was nothing spontaneous about this Boston Tea Party—it had all been carefully planned.

Carefully planned—and its inevitable results foreseen. For by this outrageous act of defiance colonial "patriots" hoped to provoke the British government into rash reprisals. And they succeeded beyond their fondest expectations.

The news of the Tea Party arrived in England late in January 1774 and caused an uproar. The British government had been openly assailed—for the East India Company had only been carrying out Parliament's orders in shipping their tea to America. The response in England was drastic—and surprisingly unanimous. Those who had all along urged that Parliament "take a strong hand" with the colonies were now able to scream "We told you so" to the rest. Those who had been friends of America were at a loss how to justify such wanton lawlessness, such impudence, such vandalism. More than £15,000 worth of tea had been ruined, and this attack upon property seemed to strike some deep psychological nerve, even among the British masses. The Great Commoner, William Pitt, always a supporter of colonial pretensions, was now forced to confess, "The violence committed upon the tea cargo is certainly criminal; nor would it be a real kindness to Americans to adopt their passions and wild pretensions, where they manifestly violate the most indispensable ties of civilized society." Benjamin Franklin, colonial agent in London, was subjected to private abuse and public humiliation.

But as early as 1772, George III had written to Lord North, in regard to the colonies: "I have also therefor looked forward to a time of war." And historians have since speculated about just who was provoking whom in Boston Harbor that cold December 16 when the tea went overboard.

Certainly the entire tendency of the king's administration was to bring colonial issues to a head when the time was ripe, and then settle them permanently—by force, if necessary. There is reason to think that by 1774 both George III and his ministers considered the time ripe. Discontent at home had abated, opposition was scattered, and the king's political machine controlled Parliament. In any event, within a few weeks, and with little debate, Parliament, at the king's bidding, passed a series of measures (by thumping majorities) designed to show the colonial vandals just who ran the empire. In England these measures were known, generally, as "Coercive Acts"; in America they would soon be dubbed the "Intolerable Acts." If the Sons of Liberty had wanted a showdown, Parliament now obliged.

First, as a punitive measure, it passed the Boston Port Act. By the terms of this law the port of Boston was closed and sealed against any and all commerce whatsoever. It would stay sealed until such time as its citizens rendered "satisfaction" for the tea they'd destroyed and the king personally decided "that peace and obedience to the laws" had been restored. To enforce this law, a squadron of the Royal Navy was dispatched to blockade the harbor, and the Boston garrison of two regiments was increased to five, under the command of General Thomas Gage. And to make certain that Bostonians understood that theirs was now an occupied city, a Quartering Act provided that British troops there should be housed in civilian homes. The Government and Administration of Justice Act, which followed, altered the entire government of Massachusetts Bay Colony. Henceforth the colonial council would be appointed by the royal governor. Its members, as well as all judges, marshals, sheriffs, and justices of the peace would hold office only during the king's pleasure. Colonial town meetings were forbidden to debate constitutional issues, and the Committees of Correspondence were declared illegal. In short, the Coercive Acts assumed that *all* the people of the Bay Colony shared the guilt of the few dozen who had actually destroyed the tea; by implication, Parliament was declaring Massachusetts to be in a state of rebellion.

Unrelated to the so-called Coercive Acts, but just as infuriating to colonial opinion was the Quebec Act, passed by Parliament on June 22, 1774. The act extended the boundary of the Quebec colony south to the Ohio River (where the French had always said it should go). This automatically dismissed the claims of Massachusetts, Virginia, and other seaboard colonies to their western lands. It also automatically ruined several American land-speculation companies. But that was not all. What really stirred American outrage was the fact that His Majesty's government announced that it would not interfere with French laws and customs in Quebec and confirmed all the rights of the Catholic Church there. This was, of course, a landmark of imperial tolerance and foresightedness for which the British government should have been commended. But to the American heirs of Puritanism the Quebec Act was the thin edge of the wedge of "popery." Sam Adams had always warned that George III was secretly planning to establish Catholicism in the New World—and here it was! Protestant ministers throughout the colonies warned their congregations that they would soon be rotting in the dungeons and torture chambers of the Inquisition. The highly combustible fuel of religious hatred was now thrown upon the spreading fire of colonial discontent.

Parliament's "Intolerable Acts" proved self-justifying; they created the widespread rebellion they were designed to repress. Sons of Liberty organizations and Committees of Correspondence in Massachusetts, which already dominated the colonial assembly, now took over local town governments throughout the colony. Royal officials, from the governor to the humblest sheriff, were forced to take refuge in Boston, where they could enjoy the protection of the local garrison; elsewhere, government passed into the hands of the "patriots." By the fall of 1774, Massachusetts was virtually independent, governed now by an illegally elected "convention." And, of course, the Committees of Correspondence had not been backward in appealing for help from other colonies.

To the surprise even of the Bostonians, the other colonies responded handsomely, pouring in food and money for the relief of the blockaded town. From Pennsylvania, New York, and New Jersey came wagonloads of flour; from the Carolinas came £2,700 worth of other provisions; from Virginia came more than 8,500 bushels of corn and wheat. And, of equal help in these trying times, from all the colonies came resolutions of support and solidarity.

This continent-wide movement to help Boston provided

yet another means by which "patriots" gained control in the various colonies. Help for the New Englanders was organized by the Committees of Correspondence. Moderate citizens moved by personal feelings of sympathy for suffering Bostonians now found themselves leagued with political militants. By supporting "treasonable" Boston, were they not themselves committing treason against the king? The method is familiar; we have seen it operate in our own day. Rebels wishing to undermine governmental authority first commit some violent or outrageous action to which any government *must* respond. But government is generally clumsy and can almost always be counted upon to *over-react*. This over-reaction may very well outrage moderate opinion, which will thus find itself in sympathy with the "persecuted" rebels. Moderates and rebels together may then provoke yet another over-reaction by government. In this process moderates may become rebels themselves, and a new, wider base of revolutionary activity is thereby created. We may pride ourselves that this technique was first developed in colonial America.

From Virginia, besides corn and wheat, came a resolution passed by its assembly (meeting in defiance of Royal Governor Dunmore's order to dissolve) that "an attack made upon one of our sister Colonies . . . is an attack made on all British America." Under the leadership of Patrick Henry, the Lee brothers, and Thomas Jefferson, the Virginia Committees of Correspondence issued a call for the convening of a congress of representatives from all the colonies to consider the whole situation. Response was enthusiastic, and on September 5, 1774, the First Continental Congress met at Philadelphia.

The fifty-five members of this Congress had been chosen outside the normal, legal constitutional channels in twelve of the colonies (Georgia, under the thumb of its royal governor, sent no delegates). They had been elected by special "conventions" or self-appointed "committees." Needless to say, these groups were led and dominated by members of the Committees of Correspondence and the Sons of Liberty. Thus these underground organizations took their first steps toward public responsibility, assuming quasi-legal governmental powers.

Most of the famous colonial leaders, like Sam and John Adams, Richard Henry Lee, Paul Revere, Thomas Jefferson, and the rest had been elected to the Congress. But in dealing with their fellow delegates, they soon found that colonial opinion, while it would support Massachusetts against the crown, wanted no part of anything remotely resembling a separation from Great Britain. Seeking to accommodate moderate opinion, some delegates proposed a plan whereby an American parliament would be established, parallel to the British Parliament. Each would enjoy a veto over acts of the other relating to America. Adams and Jefferson went further, advocating the kind of imperial relationship which, a hundred and fifty years later, led to the creation of the British Commonwealth of Nations, with independent dominion status for its members.

But Congress adopted neither of these proposals. It had met, after all, to consider the Massachusetts problem and, in the end, adopted a set of resolutions proposed by Suffolk County, Massachusetts, patriots. These Suffolk Resolves, declaring the "Intolerable Acts" null and void, urged Massachusetts citizens to arm themselves and form a "free state" until such time as the acts might be rescinded. Conservative delegate Joseph Galloway of Pennsylvania described Congress's adoption of these resolutions as "an act of war against Great Britain."

Undeterred, Congress proceeded to issue a Declaration of Rights stating that all Americans were entitled to all English liberties. It then adopted a new non-importation agreement, which called upon all Americans to cut off imports from and exports to Britain. Called "The Association," this non-intercourse agreement was to be supervised and enforced by local committees. Showing themselves as Puritanical as almost all later revolutionary assemblies, the Congress also voted to "discourage every species of extravagance and dissipation, especially all horse-racing, and all kinds of gaming, cock-fighting, exhibitions of shews, plays, and other expensive diversions and entertainments," including fancy funerals. They also voted to stop drinking imported tea and wines. But, to the relief, no doubt, of many of the delegates, nothing was said about rum. Having accomplished all this, Congress rose on October 26, 1774, after resolving to meet again the following May 10, if by that time their grievances had not been redressed.

What this First Continental Congress had been grappling with, basically, was the problem of state power. As Lenin was to observe of a much later revolutionary movement, the problem of political power in the state is the central question of any revolution. There cannot be two powers in the state; one only must rule. In American terms this meant that colonials must decide whether they would have Parliament or their own assemblies hold power. The Congress of 1774, reflecting general colonial opinion, wanted it both ways; they wanted to remain within the British Empire (in which they could only be subject to parliamentary control), yet independent of it in all matters which affected immediate colonial interests. No compromise was really possible here; but Americans did not yet realize that.

Now, throughout the colonies, Committees of Public Safety which had evolved from the old Committees of Correspondence and Sons of Liberty groups, took the law into their own hands. They had sworn to enforce The Association. They also undertook to see that Congress's ban on "diversions and entertainments" was strictly observed. Their methods were brutal—and scaled in accordance with the offense. If you did not observe The Association, the first thing that happened to you was that you were publicly "exposed, to the end that all such foes of the rights of British America may be publicly known and universally condemned as the enemies of American liberties." In other words, you were publicly branded a traitor. But a traitor to what? To an illegally self-appointed body of people who called themselves a Committee of Public Safety? Were *they* not the traitors? Had *they* not committed treason against the king and the British government? There was no nation, no colonial "state," no recognizable governmental authority in America which could legally claim your allegiance or "due submission" *except* that of England.

But if you persisted in these views, you could expect much worse than simple "public exposure." You would be tarred and feathered and ridden out of town on a rail and your property destroyed. You were the helpless target of any and all outrages. And all because you preferred the legally constituted authority of Parliament to the snooping and mindless violence of some local vigilante committee. New York clergyman Samuel Seabury, although himself a foe of the "Intolerable Acts," refused to kowtow to the committees "chosen by the weak, foolish, turbulent part of the . . . people. I will not. If I must be enslaved, let it be by a King at least, and not by a parcel of upstart, lawless committeemen!" For these words, Seabury's writings were publicly burned and he himself denounced as an enemy of mankind.

It was during the months of The Association that American political opinion polarized into "patriot" and "loyalist" extremes. Many of the better educated, wealthier, more conservative colonials were now forced by events to make a choice like Seabury's. They did not conceive of themselves as supporting a tyrannical king against a liberty-loving people. On the contrary, they thought of themselves as fighting to preserve the ancient rights and liberties of loyal British subjects against the rough tyranny of mob rule.

At the very moment that the Continental Congress moved to adjourn for the winter, Parliament was in the midst of an election campaign. British Parliaments (unless turned out earlier by the king) sat for seven years. The Parliament which had passed the Coercive Acts had one year to run. But the "king's friends" clique decided to take advantage of the general outrage over the Boston Tea Party to call for new elections. Their calculations were correct; in the Parliament which met on November 29, 1774, the "king's friends" increased their number to 321—an absolute majority of the 558 seats in the House of Commons. Having received this impressive electoral mandate for repression in the colonies, George III dispatched a note to Lord North in which he pronounced New England to be "in a state of rebellion." "Blows must decide," the king observed. "We must either master them or totally leave them to themselves and treat them as aliens." Whoever else might be confused about the indivisibility of state power, George III was not.

There were, however, other voices in England. William Pitt, now white-haired and looking, as an observer reported, "like an old Roman Senator, rising with the dignity of age, yet speaking with the fire of youth," addressed the House of Lords in January 1775, demanding a policy of reconciliation with the Americans. "What is our right to persist in such cruel and vindictive measures against that loyal and respectable people?" he asked. "Years, perhaps ages, will not heal the wounds," he warned. And during the same debate the Duke of Richmond declared: "You may spread fire, sword and desolation, but that will not be government. . . . No people can ever be made to submit to a form of government they say they will not receive."

The king was perfectly right, of course; Massachusetts was in a state of outright rebellion. General Gage had dissolved the colonial assembly, but that body, dubbing itself now the provincial congress, was meeting under the presidency of John Hancock and the direction of Sam Adams in the town of Concord. It was comporting itself in all respects just like a legal government: appointing judges, sheriffs, and other officials, passing laws, organizing a militia of local farmers (who styled themselves Minutemen on the assumption that they could be ready for battle on one minute's notice), and levying taxes. The provincial congress did, in fact, rule all of Massachusetts except for British-occupied Boston. Here was truly that dual power within the state which George III knew in his bones to be fatal. On the motion of Lord North, Parliament recognized

realities on February 2, 1775, when it formally adopted a resolution declaring the existence of a state of rebellion in Massachusetts.

Three weeks later a letter was prepared with instructions
for General Gage in Boston. He was advised "to defend the
Constitution and restore the vigor of government." A small
force, if used against the colonials now, might be more effective
than a larger army thrown against them after they had acquired "confidence from discipline." "The first and most essential step . . . toward re-establishing government," the letter
continued, "would be to arrest the principal actors and abettors
in the provincial congress," even though such a step might well
be "a signal for hostilities, yet . . . it will surely be better
that they should be brought on, upon such ground, than in a
riper state of rebellion." General Thomas Gage was known to
be friendly toward Americans. He genuinely liked them—had,
in fact, taken one to be his wife. But the general was, first and
foremost, a professional soldier. He could be counted upon to
carry out his orders. The letter of instruction was dispatched in
the brig *Nautilus,* sailing from Plymouth on March 13, 1775.

On the same day the North cabinet was preparing Gage's
letter of instruction, another letter was being written by rebel
agitator Joseph Warren in Boston to a friend in London. "It is
not yet too late to accommodate the dispute amicably," he
observed. "But . . . if once General Gage should lead his
troops into the country, with design to enforce the late Acts of
Parliament, Great Britain may take her leave . . . of all
America."

Meantime, the subject of these instructions and specula-
tions had not been inactive. Seeking to spy out the lay of the
land around Boston, General Gage dispatched a secret agent
named John Howe into the countryside. When he returned to
Boston, Howe recounted his meeting with an old man and his
wife who lived in a small house beside the road to Concord.
The old man was cleaning a gun when Howe walked in. "I
asked him," Howe reported, "what he was going to kill, as he

was so old, I should not think he could take sight at any game; he said there was a flock of redcoats at Boston, which he expected would be here soon; he meant to try and hit some of them, as he expected they would be very easy marks. I asked the old man how he expected to fight; he said: 'Open field fighting, or any other way to kill them redcoats!' I asked him how old he was; he said, 'Seventy-seven, and never was killed yet.' I asked him if there were any tories nigh there; he said there was one tory house in sight, and he wished it was in flames. The old man says, 'Old woman, put in the bullet pouch a handful of buckshot, as I understand the English like an assortment of plums!' "

The brig *Nautilus,* after an uneventful and speedy voyage, dropped her anchor amid the assembled warships in Boston Harbor on April 14, 1775.

### THE WAY IT WAS:

*"A very unusual time for firing . . ."*

"On the evening of the 18th, about 9 o'clock, I learned there was a large detachment going from the garrison, on which I immediately resolved to go with them. And meeting a few men in the street fully accoutered, I followed them and embarked at the Magazine Guard and landed near Cambridge where I joined Major Pitcairn, who I understood was to command next to Colonel Smith.

"Here we remained for two hours, partly waiting for the rest of the detachment and for provisions. About half an hour after two in the morning of the 19th we marched, Major Pitcairn commanding in front the light infantry. . . .

"A little after we were joined by Lieutenant Grant of the Royal Artillery who told us the country he was afraid, was alarmed, of which we had little reason to doubt, as we heard several shots, it being between three and four in the morning—

a very unusual time for firing. We were joined by Major Mitchel, Captain Cochrane, Captain Lumm and several other gentlemen, who told us the whole country was alarmed and they had galloped for their lives, or words to that effect; that they had taken Paul Rivierre, but was obliged to let him go after having cut his girth and stirrups. A little after a fellow came out of a cross road galloping. Mr. Adair and I called to him to stop, but he galloped off as hard as he could, upon which Mr. Simms, Surgeon's Mate of the 43rd Regiment, who was on horseback, pursued him and took him a great way in front. A little after I met a very genteel man riding in a carriage they called a sulky, who assured me there were 600 men assembled at Lexington with a view of opposing us. . . . I waited with him until Major Pitcairn came up with the division, to whom he repeated much the same as he did to me. Then going on in front again, I met, coming out of a cross road, another fellow galloping; however, hearing him sometime before, I placed myself so that I got hold of the bridle of his horse and dismounted him. Our guide seemed to think that this was a very material fellow and said something as if he had been a member of the Provincial Congress.

"A little while after this I mounted a horse I had, and Mr. Adair went in a chaise. It began to be daylight, and we met some men with a wagon of wood who told us there were odds of 1,000 men at Lexington and added that they would fight us. Here we waited for some time, but seeing nothing of the division, I rode to the left about half a mile to see if I could fall in with them, but could see nothing of them. However, I saw a vast number of the country militia going over the hill with their arms to Lexington and met one of them whom I obliged to give up his firelock and bayonet, which I believe he would not done so easily but from Mr. Adair coming up.

"On this, we turned back the road we came, and found the division who was halted in consequence of the intelligence the man in the sulky gave them, in order to make a disposition by advancing men in front and on the flanks to prevent a surprise. I went on with the front party which consisted of a sergeant and six or eight men. I shall observe here that the road before you go into Lexington is level for about 1,000 yards. Here we saw shots fired to the right and left of us, but as we heard no hissing of balls, I conclude they were to alarm the body that was there of our approach.

"On coming within gun shot of the village of Lexington, a fellow from the corner of the road on the right hand, cocked his piece at me, but burnt priming. I immediately called to Mr. Adair and the party to observe this circumstance which they did and I acquainted Major Pitcairn of it immediately. We still went on further when three more shots were fired at us, which we did not return, and this is the sacred truth as I hope for mercy. These three shot were fired from a corner of a large house to the right of the church. When we came up to the main body, which appeared to exceed 400 in and about the village, who were drawn up in a plain opposite to the Church, several officers called out, 'Throw down your arms, and you shall come to no harm,' or words to that effect.

"They refusing to act instantaneously, the gentlemen who were on horseback rode in amongst them of which I was one, at which instant I heard Major Pitcairn's voice call out, 'Soldiers, don't fire, keep your ranks, form and surround them.' Instantly some of the villains who got over the hedge fired at us, which our men for the first time returned, which set my horse a-going who galloped with me down a road above 600 yards, among the middle of them before I turned him. In returning, a vast number who were in a wood to the right of the Grenadiers fired at me, but the distance was so great I only heard the Whistling of the Balls, but saw a great number of people in the wood. In consequence of their discovering themselves, our Grenadiers gave them a smart fire. I shall take the liberty of observing here that it is very unlikely that our men should have fired for some time, otherwise they must have hurt their own officers who galloped in amongst this arm'd mob. Our men kept up their fire, and on my coming up Colonel Smith turned to me and asked, 'Do you know where a drum is,' which I found, who immediately beat to arms, when the men ceased firing.

"We marched quietly from this to Concord, only seeing some horsemen on the tops of the heights with no other view, I suppose, than to know our number and make the cowardly disposition (which they did afterwards) with a view to murder us all."

William Sutherland
Lieutenant, 38th Regiment

"During the whole of the march from Lexington, the Rebels kept an incessant irregular fire from all points at the column, which was more galling as our flanking parties, which at first were placed at sufficient distances to cover the march of it, were at last, from the different obstructions they occasionally met with, obliged to keep almost close to it. Our men had very few opportunities of getting good shots at the Rebels, as they hardly ever fired but under cover of some stone wall, from behind a tree, or out of a house; and the moment they had fired they lay down out of sight until they had loaded again, or the column had passed. In the road indeed in our rear, they were most numerous, and came pretty close, frequently calling out, *'King Hancock forever.'*

"Many of them were killed in the houses on the road side from whence they fired at us; in some, seven or eight men were destroyed. Some houses were forced open in which no person could be discovered, but when the column had passed, numbers sallied forth from some place in which they had lain concealed, fired at the rear guard, and augmented the numbers which followed us. If we had had time to set fire to those houses many rebels must have perished in them, but as night drew on, Lord Percy thought it best to continue the march. Many houses were plundered by the soldiers, notwithstanding the efforts of the officers to prevent it. I have no doubt that this inflamed the Rebels, and made many of them follow us farther than they

otherwise would have done. By all accounts some soldiers who
stayed too long in the houses, were killed in the very act of
plundering by those who lay concealed in them."

Frederick Mackenzie
Lieutenant, 23rd Regiment

Indians and Early Settlers—*"And when the Long Knives came to these shores we took them by the hand . . ."*

"Boston Massacre"—*Twenty men of the main guard were called out.*

Samuel Adams — *His background fitted him perfectly for his task.*

Thomas Paine — *". . . some mortifying disappointment is rankling at heart."*

George Washington—
*He rarely found anything amusing.*

Benjamin Franklin —
*His deep cunning was effectively disguised behind an aged, benign face.*

Lexington Green—". . . *some of the villains fired at us.*"

Retreat from Concord—". . . *in the road indeed in our rear, they were most numerous . . .*"

Battle of Long Island—*The Americans broke and fled in wild disorder.*

Franklin at Versailles—*His gallantry to the ladies . . . soon assumed scandalous proportions.*

*Bonhomme Richard* vs. *Serapis*—*"I have not yet begun to fight!"*
Battle of Cowpens (below)—*When loyalist and rebel Americans met in battle, no quarter was given or asked.*

Washington bids farewell to his officers at Fraunces' Tavern, New York—". . . *then they embraced each other in silence.*"

# 6 | "Independence, Like a Torrent . . ."

*The madness of independence has spread from colony to colony, till order is lost and government despised, and all is filled with mis-rule, uproar, violence and confusion.* –Dr. Samuel Johnson

General Gage had simply tried to carry out his instructions. On the night of April 18–19 he'd dispatched a column of light infantry to try to nab colonial leaders and seize rebel munitions supplies supposed to be stored at Lexington and Concord. The raid was a failure because rebel spies and couriers like Paul Revere and William Dawes outraced the British regulars to their objectives. Rebel munitions were carted away and such rebel leaders as John Hancock and Sam Adams (both hidden in a house only half a mile from Lexington Green) made good their escape. The march back to Boston had been a bloody disaster for the raiding party and for a relief column sent out to help them. Hundreds, perhaps thousands, of Minutemen farmers lined the roads, hiding behind boulders and rock walls and trees, taking potshots at the marching regiments, and then disappearing into the woods. Lord Hugh Percy, commanding the relief column, reported 224 casualties in killed, wounded, and missing when, at last, his harassed regulars regained the safety of Boston.

News of the fighting was carried swiftly to all parts of the colonies by special dispatch riders, who reached Philadelphia in four days, Richmond, Virginia, in ten, and South Carolina in fifteen. Everywhere an uproar ensued. The version put out by

master propagandist Sam Adams on behalf of the Massachusetts provincial congress was perfectly designed to strengthen
the rebel cause. A strong detachment of British regulars, he
wrote, had set out to harass and subdue the innocent farmers in
the towns outside Boston. But the farmers had driven these
brutal marauders back into their fortified city with severe
losses. God had, no doubt, defended the peaceful inhabitants of
Massachusetts and struck terror into the hearts of their adversaries who "fled" before them.

Emboldened by this news of victory, Committees of Public Safety throughout the colonies now stepped forward (where
they had not already done so) to assume full powers of local
and colonial government. Royal governors and other officials
took refuge on British warships. In Virginia and the Carolinas
fighting broke out between "patriots" and loyalists (who were
quickly subdued). Outside Boston itself thousands of armed
countryfolk gathered. Barricades were erected and manned on
the roads and hills overlooking the city, and within a matter of
days General Gage and his regiments were besieged by a vast
horde of undisciplined but very determined Minutemen.

Not only did the provincial congress's version of what had
happened create a furor in the colonies; their dispatches
reached London eleven days before General Gage's official report and aroused consternation there. The Paris press gleefully
carried full accounts of the defeat of the royal troops, and even
in distant Venice newspapers carried stories of *la grande
scaramùccia a Concordia* (the big skirmish at Concord). Long
before Ralph Waldo Emerson immortalized the "embattled
farmers"; the shots fired at Concord were, indeed, "heard
round the world."

With London tabloids headlining the RUNAWAY FIGHT OF
THE REGULARS, the king's ministers were troubled, to say the
least. But not George III. This was (except for the fact that
the troops had suffered a reverse) precisely the result the king
and Lord North had anticipated from their instructions to
General Gage. "With firmness and perseverance," the king re-

assured his followers, "America will be brought to submission." Displaying that stubborn determination which served him in place of intelligence, the king insisted that "America must be a colony of England or be treated as an enemy." Pitt, Burke, Fox, and the other parliamentary liberals might waste their eloquence decrying the royal obstinacy, but Lord North had the votes, more than enough of them, to control both the House of Commons and the House of Lords. There, representing the stolid British middle classes, members would enjoy liberal oratory—but vote British interests and the king's instructions. In this they were in substantial agreement with most English opinion, which was expressed by Dr. Samuel Johnson. The great lexicographer took time off from his labors on the first English dictionary to denounce the Continental Congress as "a seditious meeting, punishable by law." Parliament overwhelmingly concurred. When, years later, Lord North was reproached for having personally "lost" the North American colonies, he reminded his accusers that "The American war . . . was the war of Parliament. There was not a step taken in it that had not the express sanction of Parliament . . . it was popular at its commencement, and eagerly embraced by the people and Parliament."

While British ministers digested the news of the fighting outside Boston, colonial delegates gathered in Philadelphia. There, on May 10, 1775, the Second Continental Congress convened. It was, without doubt, the most distinguished gathering yet assembled in North America. Sam and John Adams were there as well as John Hancock, from Massachusetts; Silas Deane and Roger Sherman from Connecticut; John Jay, Philip Schuyler, and a clutch of Livingstons from New York and New Jersey; Patrick Henry, Thomas Jefferson, George Washington, and Richard Henry Lee from Virginia; Christopher Gadsden from South Carolina; Lyman Hall from Georgia; John Dickinson, Robert Morris, and Benjamin Franklin (who had fled London to escape arrest) from Pennsylvania—and many more. Their respective journeys to Philadelphia had been in the nature of triumphal processions, with cheering crowds, glorious banquets, and patriotic demonstrations all along the way. But the gentlemen gathered in the Philadelphia Statehouse faced very serious problems of both a political and personal nature.

As no one present mentioned, but as all of them knew, they were committing treason against the British government. The penalty exacted for that crime in England had not changed since the days of King John. It was to be hanged by the neck until *not quite* dead, then to have one's bowels cut out and burned before one's eyes, and, finally, to have one's body axed into four pieces which would be left to rot upon the gallows poles as an admonition to other would-be traitors. This was the personal fate awaiting congressional delegates if they were caught. Many of them must have reflected apprehensively on that old adage, "He who draws his sword against his King must throw away the scabbard!"

As if to ceremoniously mark the passing of the point of no return, delegates were confronted, a few days after Congress opened, with several British regimental flags captured from His Majesty's garrisons at Ticonderoga and Crown Point. Upon hearing of the fighting outside Boston, it seemed, one Ethan Allen of Vermont (still a part of Massachusetts), with eighty-three rugged followers who styled themselves the "Green Mountain Boys," had crossed Lake Champlain and seized these British outposts. Fighting had been minimal. At Ticonderoga, Ethan Allen himself had simply pounded on the fort's gate and demanded its surrender "in the name of the Great Jehovah and the Continental Congress!"

The Second Continental Congress, for all the genius of its membership, was clearly schizophrenic in its decisions. On the one hand, delegates realized the imperative necessity of taking hold of events; matters must not be allowed to drift. In this spirit they voted approval of Massachusetts' rebellion and declared the mob of farmers outside Boston to be the "Army of the United Colonies."

To control and organize this undisciplined militia, Congress sent Colonel George Washington of Virginia north to take over-all command. At the same time, it authorized Benedict Arnold to lead a body of volunteers across the Maine wilderness to bring Canada into the fold as the fourteenth colony. It also established three Indian Commissions to deal with the frontier tribes, either to bring them in as allies or, at least, win their neutrality. These were all, without exception, the actions of a *sovereign* political body.

But only a tiny handful of the delegates (and an even tinier percentage of the people they represented) wished to recognize any other sovereign than His Most Gracious Majesty, King George III. Independence was a word uttered only in whispers at Philadelphia, even by such radicals as Sam Adams. To have advocated independence in the spring of 1775 would have cost Congress all its popular support. So obvious was this to delegates that they ordered the invasion of Canada, created the Continental Army, and pressed the siege of royal troops in Boston—all in the name of the king!

In order to justify this apparently contradictory policy, Congress issued a "Declaration on the Causes of Taking Up Arms." The work of Dickinson and Jefferson, this curious document pretended to make a distinction between the king and his government. "We mean not to dissolve that union which has so long and so happily subsisted between us. . . . We have not raised armies with the ambitious designs of separation from Great Britain, and establishing independent States . . . we are reduced to the alternative of choosing an unconditional submission to the tyranny of irritated ministers or resistance by force." In this Declaration royal forces in America are always referred to as the "ministerial army." So that was it! Good King George had been misled by wicked, tyrannical ministers! As soon as the colonies, through their "manly resistance," exposed these parliamentary ogres, the king would, of course, dismiss them; their evil laws would be repealed and the empire would live happily ever after.

This dream of a benign monarch in the grip of bad advisers is not uncommon in the early stages of rebellion. One is almost reminded of the pathetic faith displayed by the humble Russian peasants in the essential goodness of their "little father," the tsar. Almost, but not quite. For the delegates to the Second Continental Congress were not humble peasants; they were extremely shrewd, sophisticated lawyers for the most part. They knew perfectly well that George and not his ministers determined colonial policy. Those who were unaware of this might have been set straight by Benjamin Franklin, fresh from London. But, of course, the Declaration was intended for mass consumption in North America and England among people who, presumably, still clung to illusions about their royal master.

But may we not detect a deeper motive here? What had happened so far? The colonial upper classes, whose immediate economic interests (in trade, business, and land speculation) had been damaged by British interference, had roused the colonial lower classes to widespread violence against British authority. They had done this by convincing them that Britain intended to establish an absolute tyranny over all Americans. The basic idea had been to use this popular violence to frighten Britain into allowing the colonial rich a free hand in their exploitation of the vast riches of an entire continent. But complete independence from Great Britain would leave those same colonial rich nakedly face to face with the masses of the poor, especially the urban poor, whose ferocity they had aroused. Independence would have meant the establishment, inevitably, of an American republic—and republics were notoriously prone to anarchy, mob rule, and the *dispossession of the rich*. John Adams gave the game away when he wrote, at this time, that there was "so much Venality and Corruption, so much Avarice and Ambition, such a Rage for Profit and Commerce among all Ranks and Degrees of Men, even in America," that he doubted whether there existed "public Virtue enough to support a Republic." All in all, there is no need to question the sincerity of those gentlemen of substance at Philadelphia who dreaded independence.

And the masses of the people? They were, and had always

considered themselves, English. True, there were now substantial minorities of Germans, Swedes, Irish, and other nationalities living in the colonies—but many of these had settled there precisely in order to enjoy the liberties of Englishmen. While their loyalty to the king could only have been skin-deep at best, they understood very well that it was English law and usage which protected them from persecution by their Anglo-Saxon neighbors, and made them full citizens of the empire. Americans were not, like Poles or Irishmen, being oppressed by foreign tyrants. Their language, their traditions, their culture—all were English. Independence meant more than a political wrench. It meant the disruption of all those "mystic chords of memory" (as Lincoln would one day call them) which bound people to their heritage. There is an awful note of wistfulness in Jefferson's draft of the Declaration of Independence: "We might have been a free and great people together."

While Congress debated, newly appointed General George Washington left Philadelphia on June 23, 1775, to take over-all command of the armed mob besieging Boston. En route, news reached him of yet another clash between the Continental Army and British troops—this one much bloodier than any that had gone before.

In May, General Gage had received reinforcements from England which brought the forces under his command up to the number of 10,000 regulars—not counting the thousands of marines and sailors of the fleet in Boston Harbor. With the new troops came Generals Sir Henry Clinton, Sir William Howe, and John Burgoyne. This imposing array of "top brass" looked around and did not like what they saw. British forces in Boston were hemmed in on all sides by colonials occupying the hills surrounding the town with the exception of the heights near Charlestown. Only the rebels' lack of artillery had saved the British army of occupation from a devastating bombardment. The first step out of this trap would be for a few regiments to occupy the Charlestown heights—especially Breed's and Bunker hills. Preparations were accordingly set afoot, and, while they were in progress, General Gage issued a proclamation (written for him by Burgoyne) to the "infatuated multitudes" who "with a preposterous parade affect to hold the army besieged." The general promised a full pardon to all who would lay down their arms, except the archvillains Samuel Adams and John Hancock.

While disregarding the proclamation, the "preposterous multitudes" had learned, through spies, of the British intention to occupy those strategic hills at Charlestown. Accordingly, on the night of June 16–17, about 3,000 colonials entrenched themselves on Breed's Hill, thereby beating the laggard British to the punch. Gage could not, of course, accept this slamming of the last door out of Boston. Warships in the harbor immediately opened a long-range cannonade upon the entrenchers. When this had no effect, several regiments were assembled to drive them out. Three times, in solid ranks, the British soldiers marched up Breed's Hill—and three times they were driven back by a blistering fire from the defenders. Only when the rebel militia ran out of ammunition did they give up their position in the face of a fourth British bayonet charge.

When the British regulars looked back down the slope they had won, they saw it littered with their dead and wounded —almost half their number were casualties. "A dear bought victory," wrote General Clinton, "another such would have ruined us." And General Gage complained, "Those people shew a spirit and conduct against us they never shewed against the French." The British, at appalling cost, had won a minor tactical victory, but the Americans had been the moral victors in this first real stand-up fight against English regulars. When Washington reached Cambridge (the rebel command post outside Boston) on July 2, he found an elated and confident 15,000 men awaiting him.

While the news of "Bunker" Hill (a mistaken identity fixed forever in American history) spread jubilation to some and apprehension to others throughout the colonies, the Continental Congress deemed the moment propitious to draw up a formal address to the king. Known as the Olive Branch Petition, it was the work of Pennsylvania's John Dickinson.

Impatient John Adams, writing to his wife, Abigail, derided the cautious Pennsylvanian and scorned his motives: "His mother said to him, 'Johnny, you will be hanged, your estate will be forfeited and confiscated, you will leave your excellent wife a widow, and your charming children orphans, beggars and infamous.' From my soul I pitied Mr. Dickinson." Congress, however, did not agree with Adams; it adopted Dickinson's petition on July 8, 1775, and sent it to England.

"Attached to your Majesty's person, family and government with all the devotion that principle and affection can inspire," declared this curious document, ". . . and deploring every event that tends in any degree to weaken them, we solemnly assure your Majesty, that we . . . most ardently desire the former harmony . . ." and so forth, and so on. The Olive Branch Petition reached London late in August—and the king refused to so much as read it. To have done so would have been to recognize, to some degree, the legitimacy of the treasonable gathering that issued it.

Besides, from George III's point of view, any and all such petitions were mere exercises in hypocrisy. British troops had been attacked at Lexington and Concord; they had been slaughtered at Bunker Hill. That traitorous, illegal, and impertinent Congress had created an army, had appointed officers to command it, had encouraged the ousting of royal governors and their councils from all the colonies, had ordered an invasion of the loyal colony of Canada, and one of its members had even gone so far as to organize a postal service which now competed with the royal mails! On August 23, 1775, the king proclaimed that a general rebellion existed throughout all North America, and that "utmost endeavours" must be made to "suppress such rebellion, and to bring the traitors to justice." A resolution to the same effect was introduced into Parliament on October 26. There ensued the usual rhetoric and flights of oratory on the part of Pitt, Fox, Burke, and the other "friends of America," but Lord North's steamroller crushed all opposition. The resolution was adopted on December 22, 1775, by a majority of more than two to one.

Passing resolutions to suppress rebellion was easy— gathering the forces necessary to do so was not. The British army in 1775 was surprisingly small, considering its imperial obligations. The army of occupation in Ireland was down to 7,500 men, there were fewer than 10,000 men stationed in England, another 7,000 were scattered in outposts from Gibraltar to the West Indies, and, of course, there were Gage's 10,000 (their numbers now reduced after Bunker Hill) cooped up in Boston. Recruiting went slowly—the miserable pay and harsh living conditions of the eighteenth-century soldier had little appeal for Englishmen. But the generals demanded men and more men. "Unless it rains men in red coats," complained General Clinton, "I know not where we are to get all we shall want."

But the king and Lord North knew—or thought they knew. They would hire mercenaries from other countries. First they tried to hire 20,000 Russians from Empress Catherine the Great. The Earl of Suffolk gleefully rubbed his hands together at this prospect. "I have been thinking about these 20,000 Russians," he remarked. "They will be charming visitors at New York and civilize that part of America wonderfully." But Catherine turned down the English request in a very abrupt and rude manner. Undaunted by this failure, the king's ministers turned to the petty German states. The rulers of these principalities were always in need of money to pay for their extravagances, and were in the habit of renting out their soldiers to foreign governments. In the end, 12,000 mercenaries were hired, principally from Hesse-Hanau and Hesse-Cassel (whence the name "Hessians"), at the going market price. This raised the predictable howl of anguish from liberals in Parliament—and even moved Frederick the Great, king of Prussia, to announce that he would make all Hessian troops marching through his dominions on their way to America pay the usual cattle tax, because they had been sold as beasts.

But Parliament, obedient to the king's will, swallowed the

pill and, as 1775 drew to a close, passed a new and comprehensive Prohibitory Act. This law repealed the Boston Port Act in order to substitute for it a declaration that prohibited all foreign trade and intercourse with any of the colonies during the course of the present rebellion. In effect, it authorized the Royal Navy to establish a blockade of the entire American coastline. When John Adams heard of Parliament's action (in March 1776), he wrote: "I know not whether you have seen the Act of Parliament call'd the restraining Act, or Prohibitory Act, or piratical Act, or plundering Act, or Act of Independency. . . . It throws thirteen colonies out of the Royal Protection, levels all distinctions, and makes us independent in spight of our supplications and entreaties."

The year 1776 was barely two weeks old when General Washington, desperately trying to organize his huge mob of poorly armed and totally undisciplined farmers outside Boston into something resembling an army, received news that Congress's invasion of Canada had ended in total disaster. General Richard Montgomery had led a force of some 1,000 New Englanders up the Hudson River and over Lake Champlain to attack Montreal. That city had surrendered on November 12, 1775. Then Montgomery marched overland to Quebec, where he met Benedict Arnold and 600 volunteers who had toiled through the Maine wilderness to reach the city. But Quebec presented as tough a problem to the besieging colonials as it had to the British nearly twenty years earlier. On New Year's Eve 1775 the combined forces of Montgomery and Arnold assaulted the citadel and were bloodily repulsed. Like Wolfe, Montgomery was killed outside Quebec's walls. Arnold waited until spring and then led a handful of demoralized survivors back through the bitter wilderness to Lake Champlain. To Washington this news meant that the British would now be able to use Canada as a base from which they might invade the thirteen colonies by the Hudson Valley route, thereby isolating New England.

The disappointment of the Canadian campaign was balanced, however, by the arrival at the end of February of several heavy cannon captured at Fort Ticonderoga. These cast-iron monsters had been inched up steep mountains, floated down treacherous streams, and sledged through the snowbound wilderness foot by toilsome foot with prodigious determination. Now they were hauled up Dorchester Heights overlooking Boston, and during the first days of March they spoke. Neither the British army in Boston nor the fleet of warships in its harbor could survive a prolonged bombardment; on March 17, 1776, the British evacuated the city. The ragged colonial militia swarmed into the town amidst the cheers of the populace (that part of the populace which had not fled with the British), but Washington, as he watched the Royal Navy's tops'ls disappear below the horizon, wondered where the British would strike next.

It was not only military success, however, which excited colonial imaginations during the winter and spring of 1776. It was a small pamphlet that had been published in Philadelphia in January. Written by a recent English immigrant named Thomas Paine, it was entitled *Common Sense,* and it was the most influential piece of writing that had yet appeared in America—perhaps the most influential that would ever appear. Going straight to the heart of the colonial dilemma, Paine called for immediate, outright independence from Great Britain. His words, intended for mass appeal, were neither subtle nor temperate; they were touched by the fire of genius.

In *Common Sense,* Paine appealed to Americans to turn their backs on the outworn institutions of Europe and to create in America a totally new kind of society. He ridiculed sentimental attachments to England and scored the institution of monarchy with withering sarcasm. How kings "came into the world so exalted above the rest, and distinguished like some new species, is worth inquiring into," he declared. One honest man was worth "all the crowned ruffians that ever lived." Reconciliation with Britain was no longer possible, and, if it were, there was no guarantee against future attempts at tyranny. "A thirst for absolute power is the natural disease of monarchy," Paine pointed out. Besides, an independent America could trade with all the world—thereby obtaining the necessary money to purchase much needed weapons and munitions.

"We have it in our power to begin the world over again," Paine wrote. "The birth day of a new world is at hand, and a race of men, perhaps as numerous as all Europe contains, are to receive their portion of freedom. . . . Independence is the only bond that can tie and keep us together. . . . The cause of America is in great measure the cause of all mankind."

Within a matter of weeks some hundred thousand copies of *Common Sense* (equivalent to a sale of a million today) were circulating through cities, towns, and villages in every colony. Washington proclaimed it "Sound doctrine and unanswerable." John Adams told his wife, Abigail, that soon the arguments of Paine would be "the common faith." Writing to her from Philadelphia, Adams reported: "Every post and every day rolls in upon us Independence like a torrent."

What Paine had accomplished in *Common Sense* was twofold. First, he had brushed aside the cobwebs of illusion from colonial eyes. The war against Great Britain could no longer be waged, in a practical sense, upon the former pretense of loyalty to the crown. Without foreign supplies and, probably, foreign aid, the colonies would lose. But no European country would risk war with the British Empire to help the colonies unless there was some assurance that the rebels really meant to maintain the struggle. Only an act of self-proclaimed independence could provide that assurance.

Secondly, Paine eloquently expressed those half-formulated, dimly envisioned dreams which were to supply a "cause" upon which colonists could unite and which would sustain them through the trying times ahead. That cause was more than independence. It was the unique opportunity to create a new, free, just society which could ignite and keep alight the flame of liberty for all mankind. Implicit in that dream was the promise that such a society would better the lot of the humble by opening the doors of equal social and economic opportunity —and it was this that aroused farmers, frontiersmen, "mechanicks," and the urban poor. Their pressure, in turn, upon the upper-class reluctant rebels in Philadelphia proved irresistible.

In those colonies where independent governments had already been established, pro-independence delegates now ousted conservatives from office. In Pennsylvania the people forced the election of a new government, which instructed its delegates to the Continental Congress to vote for independence. In North and South Carolina the story was the same. Virginia went further—she instructed her delegates to *propose* independence. Accordingly, on June 7, 1776, speaking for the Virginia delegation, Richard Henry Lee rose in Congress and moved that "these United Colonies are, and of a right ought to be, free and independent States." The ensuing debate was hard and long—there were still those in Congress who feared the ultimate results of independence. John Adams, though openly supporting the Lee motion, privately never forgave Paine for his pamphlet. "What a poor, ignorant, malicious, short-sighted, crapulous mass, is Tom Paine's *Common Sense*," he wrote. But the tide of opinion was not to be resisted. On June 11, Congress appointed a committee, consisting of Thomas Jefferson, John Adams, Benjamin Franklin, Roger Sherman, and Robert Livingston to prepare a formal declaration setting forth the reasons "which impelled us to this mighty resolution."

After the committee of five came to an agreement over the main points to be covered, it assigned Jefferson (whose writing ability was well known) to clothe the declaration "in proper dress." The Declaration of Independence, his great handiwork, was adopted (by a bare majority and with several notable abstentions) by Congress on July 2 and printed on July 4, 1776.

The Declaration took its stand upon the broad ground of natural rights. "We hold these truths to be self-evident, that all men are created equal, that they are endowed by their Creator with certain unalienable Rights, that among these are Life, Liberty, and the Pursuit of Happiness." So wrote Jefferson the slaveowner; but he, like almost all the Founding Fathers, did not really conceive that black slaves could be "men." "That to secure these Rights, Governments are instituted among Men, deriving their just Powers from the Consent of the Governed." This phrase was heartily approved by many of the same men who, in later years, would help to devise a Constitution which, in its original form, excluded the majority of the people from any share in the election of presidents or senators. "That, whenever any Form of Government becomes destructive of these Ends, it is the Right of the People to alter or to abolish it . . ." So agreed the men who would one day crush the Whisky Rebellion and Shays' uprising with the utmost severity. And yet—

And yet the Declaration of Independence remains the single most explosive revolutionary document ever written, with the possible exception of the *Communist Manifesto*. Like the *Manifesto,* it assumes that man is innately good in a state of nature, that he can and will control his social destiny, and that no shackles will ever long restrain him. Like the *Manifesto,* the Declaration of Independence also contains a long bill of grievances—directed against King George III rather than against the "ruling class." Neither of these lists of grievances is correct or, for that matter, important; the underlying faith in mankind is. In after years, wherever men fought for freedom and independence, they turned for inspiration to Jefferson's immortal words. It was by no accident that Ho Chi Minh, announcing Vietnamese independence from the French in 1946, began his own proclamation with the words: "We hold these truths to be self-evident, that all men are created equal, that they are endowed by their Creator with certain unalienable rights . . ."

THE WAY IT WAS:

*"Quebec is ours!"*

"We have heard for some time, heavy discharges of musketry and artillery in different parts of town:—we are elated with this music and shout—'Quebec is ours!' We again invite the enemy to come out from behind their covert and try our rifles, which we offer to them for sale at a very low rate. They, however, decline the offer, observing that they shortly expect them for nothing. Our main body now appears, having taken a wrong route through narrow and crooked streets, exposed to a cowardly fire from houses. We heartily cheer each other, and now prepare to storm the battery. The ladders are laid to the wall. Our gallant officers are mounting, followed by several men, when a furious discharge of musketry is let loose upon us from behind houses. In an instant we are assailed from different quarters with a deadly fire. We now find it impossible to force the battery . . .

"The battle becomes hot, and is much scattered; but we distinguish each other by hemlock sprigs previously placed in our hats. All our officers are most gallant. Betwixt every peal the aweful voice of Morgan is heard, whose gigantic stature and terrible appearance carries dismay among the foe wherever he comes. My brave captain is sublimated with the most exalted courage—he seems to be all soul, and moves as though he did not touch this earth. But whilst he is most heroically animating us with his voice and example, a ball flies into his breast and lays him dead on the spot. We have no time to weep. We are now attacked in our rear. The enemy increases momently; they call out to us to surrender, but we surrender them our bullets and retreat to the first battery. Here we maintain ourselves until 10 o'clock when, surrounded on every side, many of our officers and men slain, and no hopes of escape, we are reluctantly compelled to surrender ourselves prisoners of war after having fought manfully for more than three hours.

"The division under General Montgomery was also unsuccessful. He, together with several officers and eleven men, were killed in the beginning of the attack, and the rest retreated. He was interred with military honors by order of General Sir Guy Carleton. It was in consequence of the failure of this division that the enemy turned their full force upon us. There were about 100 killed and wounded and nearly 400 taken prisoners.

"After we were taken prisoners, we were taken to an old French College, our officers were taken from amongst us. Some rum and a biscuit apiece was given to us. We were kindly treated by both General Carleton and the people of the town until one Deway was placed over us, who sold the provisions allowed us for his own profit. But the Lord of Hosts soon delivered us out of his hands, for he was taken with the smallpox which swept him off the face of the earth. On the 31st of March a plot was laid amongst us to free ourselves. The plan was as follows: we made officers of our sergeants and formed ourselves into three divisions. The first division was to take the guard that stood over us. The second was to secure the guard at Saint John's Gate. The third, among whom was the artillery men, was to seize the cannon and turn them upon the town. Then we procured a person to go over to the army under Colonel Arnold now blockading the place and notify the Colonel of the plot and the signals to be used. But the scoundrel that knew of it informed the barracks master. The consequence was that the sergeants were all put in irons, seven to a bolt, and the privates handcuffed two and two together.

"Here we lay, wretched, and ragged, and covered with vermin, until the 8th of May when Colonel Arnold retreated up the river. Then General Carleton ordered our irons to be knocked off, and on the 6th of June his Excellency came into the jail and observed to us, that if he could depend upon our word of honor to behave peaceably and not to take up arms in future against His Majesty, he would engage to send us home. He then presented a paper purporting his request, which we all signed . . ."
                                         George Morrison
                                         Pennsylvania Rifles

# 7 | The American Crisis

*It is impossible to conquer a map.*                    —William Pitt

*It takes* citizens *to support hunger, nakedness, toil and the total want of pay.*                    –Lafayette

The trouble was, at first, that although Washington commanded some 18,000 men in and around conquered Boston, they were by no stretch of the imagination an army. Almost all were farmers who had formed local militia units in their towns and villages, electing their own officers and providing their own weapons (a mixture of muskets, carbines, shotguns, and rifles), and then marched to Boston when the news of Lexington and Concord reached them. Although the majority were New Englanders at first, their numbers were soon swollen with militiamen from every colony—all as badly armed, haphazardly led, and totally undisciplined as their Yankee brethren. Their enlistments were, generally, for no specific term—they simply intended to fight for as long as ever it took to liberate Boston and teach the bloody British a lesson. That this "rabble in arms" could have successfully besieged the king's professional regiments and then driven them from Boston was due only to the indecisiveness of royal commanders—and to a widespread English misconception as to what the fighting was all about.

In the early days of the struggle British commanders in North America conceived themselves to be putting down local rebellion and providing armed protection and assistance to that great majority of colonials who were, it was assumed, fervently loyal to the king. Boston, New York, and Philadelphia were, after all, English cities, their inhabitants His Majesty's subjects. British generals, from Gage to Cornwallis, could never believe themselves to be fighting a foreign enemy; at most they were waging a civil war against a minority of their fellow countrymen. Although the professional soldiers they commanded (the dregs of English society) were quite willing to slaughter anyone they were ordered to, and individual officers were responsible for some shocking barbarities, by and large the British commanders in North America acted with a restraint they would never have shown to a foreign enemy.

All wars are political—but none are more completely determined by political attitudes than rebellions. It was English blindness to the deeper political tides running in the colonies that had brought about armed rebellion in the first place. That same blindness was to bring ultimate defeat.

The battle for New York is an example. When General Gage's ships disappeared over the horizon after the evacuation of Boston, they headed straight for Halifax, Nova Scotia, and Gage himself for London and disgrace. He was replaced in command of the British forces in North America by Sir William Howe, who was then reinforced by British and Hessian regiments to a strength of 25,000 and a fleet of warships commanded by his brother, Admiral Richard Lord Howe. The king's ministers in London, convinced that rebellion was effectively limited only to New England, ordered the Howe brothers to seize New York, drive up the Hudson Valley to Albany, and so isolate New England from the rest of "loyal" America. Once this was accomplished, the Yankee rebels could be suppressed at leisure.

Washington required no particular military acumen to foresee this English plan, and soon after the capture of Boston he hurried his untrained mobs down to New York. At least he hurried some of them. Many of the New Englanders, having finished, as they supposed, their business with the English at Boston, saw no reason to pursue the matter further and simply went home.

This matter of enlistment—of who could be made or persuaded to fight where and when and under what terms—was
the most vexing problem Washington ever had to face. Individual militia units, generally enlisted for three or six months,
could not be made to fight outside their home colonies except
on the orders of their own legislatures. And with the British
liable to descend anywhere on the coast at any time, colonial
legislatures understandably preferred to keep their volunteer
militia units at home for local defense.

To solve this problem Congress had authorized the creation of a Continental Army. But it had limited enlistments to
one year. Regiments in this army (theoretically composed of
500 officers and men) were recruited in and named after individual states—hence such names as the "Massachusetts Line,"
or the "New Jersey Line." Unfortunately, the one-year enlistment period meant that just about the time a soldier had been
thoroughly trained he had to be granted a discharge. And no
system for the replacement of casualties in the individual regiments was ever devised.

Later, Congress attempted to induce enlistments for a
three-year period by offering large bounties—but with little
success. The truth was that Americans hated military service.
Also, the average American simply could not afford to sign up
for long enlistment periods. Congress never made any provision
for soldiers' dependents, and, unless these were to starve, men
had to go home from time to time to plant the corn or get in the
hay or harvest the wheat. Almost all historians agree that this
colonial enlistment policy (or, rather, lack of one) was a near
fatal handicap. In this, as we shall see, they are at least partly
mistaken.

If the English were, at first, confused as to the nature of
the war they were fighting, so were the Americans. While Lord
North and his colleagues conceived it their task to suppress a
small, rebellious portion of the population and "pacify" the
rest, the Americans imagined that a few more such easy victories as that of Boston would persuade the king that the cost
of conquering America was prohibitive—that the game was not

worth the candle. This, in turn, led to the strangely political battle of New York—a kind of deadly blindman's buff of mutual error.

As Washington had foreseen, the British turned up at New York on schedule. Their huge fleet of transports, protected by grim frigates and ships of the line, began debarking 25,000 English regulars and Hessian mercenaries on Staten Island during the first week of July 1776. British warships acquired complete control of New York Harbor, the East River, and the Hudson—and, since New York was a city of islands, it would seem that Washington's only possible strategy would have been instant flight. But remember the political factors underlying his decisions.

It was Washington's duty to prove to the English that the cost of suppressing the rebellion would be prohibitive. So far the rebels had badly mauled English forces only in small guerrilla-type actions, or when entrenched (as at Bunker Hill) behind all but impregnable fortifications. If now they could stand up to His Majesty's troops in open battle and (even if they lost) inflict heavy casualties, that might just turn the trick. Besides, his mob of militiamen had been dubbed the *Continental* Army—it was vital that it fight for the rebel cause at New York just as it had at Boston, if colonial unity (a fragile idea) was to be maintained.

At first Washington entrenched his men on Brooklyn Heights—hoping, perhaps, that Sir William Howe would accommodate him with yet another charge up a hill. But "Sir Billy" refused to oblige, whereupon Washington marched his men down onto the plain below the heights for a stand-up open-field fight-to-the-finish which should teach the British the hopelessness of their cause.

Unfortunately, it worked the other way. Unused to regular, open-field warfare, untrained in its essential maneuvers, and unequipped with its decisive weapon, the bayonet, the Americans broke and fled in wild disorder, leaving more than 1,000 casualties behind them. Since the British and Hessians could now close in on the rebels at their leisure, with escape from Long Island presumably blocked by the Royal Navy, the Continental Army faced annihilation.

But, surprisingly, there was no close pursuit, there was no blockade. On the night following this disastrous battle of Long Island (August 27, 1776), in a kind of eighteenth-century Dunkirk, the surviving rebel forces made good their escape across the East River into Manhattan. There, of course, they found themselves on yet another island, potentially surrounded by British warships. Again the story was the same; the Americans fled at the first British assault (Washington on horseback cursing mightily and slashing out with his sword in a vain effort to hold his men to their duty)—and again they escaped capture.

Posting himself on the northern tip of Manhattan Island, Washington built Fort Washington and manned it with 5,000 men; across the Hudson River he built Fort Lee on the Jersey Palisades and there posted another 3,000 men. His idea seems to have been to prevent a British advance up the Hudson Valley by bluff, since neither fort had the artillery necessary to command the river against British frigates. This policy of splitting his forces proved ruinous; Howe's lieutenant, General Cornwallis, captured Fort Lee, while the Hessians took Fort Washington. The remnants of the Continental Army (some 5,000 men) under Washington thereupon crossed the Hudson and fled south through New Jersey, their general object being to place themselves between the British forces and Philadelphia. Why, with at least three different golden opportunities to capture the rebel host intact, did Sir William Howe, an experienced military man, allow it to slip through his fingers?

"Sir Billy," as he was called, has been dubbed "the greatest bus-misser in English history," and certainly he was far from Napoleonic in speed and decisiveness. But at least an important part of the reason for his failure to end the rebellion at New York was the fact that Howe's military decisions were heavily influenced by political assumptions and considerations.

He had been dispatched to New York to suppress a rebellion, not to conquer a foreign country. He was to use persuasion as well as force. In his pocket he carried the king's pardon to all rebels who would lay down their arms and swear fealty to George III. It was only after congressional negotiators turned down his offer of amnesty that he had moved against the rebels in the first place. For his purposes the defeat and dispersal of the rebel army ought, he reasoned, to be sufficient.

The exertion of British military force was intended to frighten, to chastise, to *persuade* Americans of their folly—those Americans who were rebels. For Sir William, like his superiors in London, clung to the belief that the great majority of the colonial population was loyal. Disperse the armed malcontents, hang a few of their leaders, capture their preposterous "Congress," and show the rest who was boss—that was the way to deal with rebellion. Thus Howe's military policy suffered not only from his personal sloth but from the haziness of his political analysis—a haziness which was shared by almost all British military and political leaders and which would eventually cost them an empire.

If Howe failed to learn a lesson from events in New York (the pursuit of Washington's defeated remnants across New Jersey was carried out in a very leisurely fashion by Cornwallis), Washington did not. It was now very apparent to him that he must never again pit his raw recruits against British regulars in open battle unless they enjoyed a crushing superiority in numbers. Such a superiority could only be hoped for in isolated encounters with fragments of the British army. Putting the icy Delaware River between himself and his pursuers, Washington established winter quarters where the tattered remnants of his army might lick their wounds, while Howe busied himself chastising rebels in Rhode Island.

Defeat before Quebec, defeat at New York. Now the British occupied almost all of New Jersey and could capture Philadelphia whenever they chose. It was at this time that Washington wrote, in unconscious echo of Wolfe before

Quebec: "No man, I believe, ever had a greater choice of difficulties . . ." Not only did he command a still untrained, badly equipped, and now defeated army, but the outlook for the rebel cause generally seemed grim.

A symptom of this was the fact that very few supplies of any kind reached the Continental Army—not because they were unavailable, but because the mass of the American people seemed indifferent to the soldiers' plight. Another symptom was the fact that British forces occupying New Jersey received, in many cases, a warm welcome; nowhere was there any kind of popular resistance. Congress, debating endlessly and passing lofty resolutions, could not seem to arouse the great majority of Americans to support the struggle.

In December 1776 appeared Tom Paine's new pamphlet, *The Crisis,* with its somber analysis of the rebel position: "These are the times that try men's souls. The summer soldier and the sunshine patriot will, in this crisis, shrink from the service of their country; but he that stands it now deserves the love and thanks of man and woman. Tyranny, like hell, is not easily conquered . . ." The truth was that aside from the highly vocal extremists on either side—the rebels and the loyalists—most Americans remained neutral. They watched and waited and would commit themselves only to the side which appeared certain to win.

So deep was rebel depression as 1776 drew to its close that Washington realized he must act. It was not enough to preserve a Continental Army in being. That army must be seen to fight and, at least occasionally, win, if the rebel cause was to maintain its credibility. Besides, a very high percentage of his soldiers' enlistments were due to end with the year. If he did not move at once, Washington realized, he might not have an army left to move at all after January 1, 1777. Casting about for a chance to strike a reasonably safe yet effective blow, he seized upon the opportunity offered by the Hessian encampment at Trenton on the other side of the Delaware River.

To Colonel Johann Gottlieb Rall and his Hessian regiments (about 1,200 men) occupying the advanced British outpost at Trenton, the campaign of 1776 was over. After all, Sir William Howe himself had proclaimed it to be over on December 13, and that should have been that. Since then, when not engaged in their favorite occupation of looting civilian homes, the German troops under Rall's command had spent most of their time drinking up the supply of local rum. Rall himself consumed large quantities every night and spent the following mornings in painful hangovers. On Christmas Day the colonel and his men got especially drunk—and their hangovers the following dawn would be the worst they would ever know. For at daybreak on December 26, Washington and about 2,400 men, who had ferried themselves over the Delaware River the previous night, fell upon the sleeping Germans with muskets and cannon. The fighting was over in minutes—Colonel Rall and some forty-five of his men were killed (for a loss of just five American lives), a handful escaped, and the rest—about 800 stunned and unbelieving Hessians—were taken prisoner.

This blow accomplished in the political sphere all that Washington had hoped. The Hessians, marched through the streets of Philadelphia, made a superb propaganda trophy. As news of this success spread through the colonies, it lifted rebel spirits everywhere. The Continental Army, it seemed, really did exist; the cause was far from lost. New Jersey and Pennsylvania recruits now flocked to the rebel standard (a flag with thirteen red and white stripes with a British Union Jack in the upper left-hand corner), and some regiments re-enlisted. In distant London, Lord George Germain wailed, "All our hopes were blasted by the unhappy affair at Trenton."

Now, with his forces grown to 5,000 men, Washington started a campaign to reconquer New Jersey. His policy was to hit the British garrisons scattered through that state and then run before any large body of regulars could assemble to catch him. A British garrison was defeated at Princeton, and part of it captured. Later, American raiding parties captured Hackensack, Elizabeth, and Newark. Before going into winter quarters

at Morristown, New Jersey, early in 1777, Washington's guerrilla tactics had been triumphantly vindicated. In a brilliant
campaign lasting just three weeks he compelled the British to
call in their scattered Jersey garrisons to the safety of New
York. And this time the Jersey farmers, maddened by the
brutal and rapacious conduct of English and Hessian occupation forces, swarmed forth to help the Continentals. This, in
turn, magnified the political victory.

For the Continental Army was not only the core and symbol of rebel resistance. It had another and, perhaps, equally
important function that is too frequently overlooked. The Continental Army was the single most important generator of rebel
sentiments and commitment in North America.

Those who passed through this harsh "radicalization
machine" (or fought alongside it, as in the case of local militia) came out, for the most part, confirmed in rebel convic-
tions. Nothing so marvelously clarifies a man's mind as the
whistle of bullets and the example of comradely sacrifice.
When Continental veterans returned to their home localities,
they were the most effective of rebel propagandists. They were
seeds of extremist sentiment planted in receptive soil. This is
why short-term enlistments and the constant drain of men
from the Continental Army, while deplored by military historians as nearly fatal, were extremely advantageous politically. The Continental Army was also the Continental School
of Rebellion—and its classes graduated with gratifying frequency.

While Sir William Howe passed a pleasant winter in New
York with his mistress and his somewhat bewildered troops,
one of his officers, Major General John Burgoyne, sold Lord
North and the rest of the king's ministers on a new plan to
suppress the North American rebellion. What he proposed was
to lead an army by way of Lake Champlain and the Hudson
River to the invasion of northern New York and New England.
At the same time, Sir William Howe would advance up to
Albany, thereby cutting the colonies into several sections,

which could then be pacified at leisure. Thousands of Mohawk
Indians and loyalists would also be enlisted in central New
York to aid both armies. Militarily sound, this plan foundered,
as others had, on political oversight.

What the plan overlooked was the existence in Vermont
(now a self-proclaimed independent state as yet unrecognized
by Congress because the area was still claimed by Massachusetts and New York) of many thousands of grim New England
farmers of the rebel persuasion. Despite their earlier capture of
Fort Ticonderoga, these Green Mountain Boys had evidently
made insufficient impression in London—a matter they would
soon correct. In any event, in the first week of June 1777,
"Gentleman Johnny" Burgoyne, commanding 4,000 British
regulars, 3,000 German mercenaries, and some 1,000 Canadian
militia and Indians, started south from the St. Lawrence. Behind him stretched a long and cumbersome baggage train
thronging with officers' wives and children, prostitutes, and
other camp followers. As they toiled slowly through the wilderness, Burgoyne composed eloquent speeches to lift their
spirits: "Warriors! Go forth in the might and valor of your
cause . . ." et cetera.

But while Burgoyne's host floundered south, Sir William
Howe's forces did not press up the Hudson to Albany, despite
the plan. Stung by his failure in New Jersey, Sir Billy had
decided to erase that disgrace by seizing the rebel capital,
Philadelphia. But this time he would avoid the pestilential
Jerseys by a seaborne landing. Accordingly, 18,000 of his
troops were loaded onto transports early in June to proceed
under convoy to Chesapeake Bay. This maneuver consumed
days and weeks—and while Howe's men huddled miserable
and seasick in their transports, Burgoyne plunged ahead to
keep an appointment in Albany which, unknown to him, had
already been canceled.

Gathering to oppose Gentleman Johnny was the so-called
American Northern Army commanded by General Horatio
Gates, a recent English immigrant to Virginia whom Washing-

ton had made adjutant general of the Continental Army. A slow and somewhat dim-witted commander, Gates was fortunate to have the assistance of Brigadier General (he'd been promoted) Benedict Arnold (a man he detested), whose courage and brilliant tactical sense more than made up for the general's shortcomings.

At first Burgoyne's march went smoothly enough. His vast host had no difficulty in capturing Fort Ticonderoga from a small American garrison and then pushing on to Fort Edward on the Hudson. There he waited for food and supplies to reach him from Canada—it took nearly five weeks to carry one month's provisions for the army down from the St. Lawrence. While waiting for food, Burgoyne made two diversions, neither successful.

One, under Colonel Barry St. Leger, marched from Oswego into the middle of the Mohawk country to besiege American-held Fort Stanwix. St. Leger had been assured that his arrival would signalize a large turnout of Mohawk Indians and loyalists. The Indians turned out—but so did a much larger force of angry New York Dutch farmers commanded by gruff old General Nicholas Herkimer. The New Yorkers were ambushed by the Mohawks at Oriskany, but a smaller force under Benedict Arnold spread false rumors which panicked the Indian braves. On August 22, St. Leger gave up his attempt to take Fort Stanwix and retired to Canada.

Burgoyne's second expedition went into Vermont in search of food—375 dismounted German heavy dragoons under Colonel Baum and 400 Canadians and Indians. This party never even reached the Vermont line, for, as Gentleman Johnny complained, "Wherever the King's forces point, militia to the number of three or four thousand assemble in a few hours." The militia in this case were an angry swarm of several thousand Green Mountain Boys under the command of General John Stark, a veteran of Bunker Hill. The Vermonters fell upon Burgoyne's raiders outside Bennington and killed or captured every one of them.

Undaunted by these losses, Burgoyne pushed on toward Saratoga and his personal rendezvous with destiny.

Meanwhile, Howe's 18,000 seasick regulars had debarked from their transports near the head of Chesapeake Bay. There they were only fifty miles from Philadelphia. Washington, with 12,000 men (nearly a third were local militia), had, for political reasons, no choice but to fight for the capital. But Howe brushed the Americans aside at Brandywine Creek (September 11, 1777), and two weeks later marched into Philadelphia with bands playing. Congress had already fled the doomed city to establish itself at Lancaster, Pennsylvania. Washington, his forces much reduced by the desertions which followed every defeat, attacked Howe again at Germantown on October 4, but was badly mauled. The British, it seemed, had learned caution, and Howe handled his army with skill.

Unable to fight another battle with his now demoralized troops, Washington led them into winter quarters at Valley Forge, Pennsylvania. There they erected rude log huts and prepared as best they could for the long, cold months that lay ahead. But two weeks after Germantown came electrifying news from the north.

General Burgoyne's army had reached Saratoga in mid-September only to find itself hopelessly surrounded by a people in arms. Thousands of Green Mountain Boys poured over into New York to join Gates' Northern Army, which was now swollen to more than 20,000. General Benjamin Lincoln, with yet more of the New England militia, cut off Burgoyne's line of supply—and retreat. Gentleman Johnny tried to fight his way out of the trap, but was beaten back in the battles of Bemis Heights and Freeman's Farm—largely through the energy and daring of Benedict Arnold. Finally, with only 5,000 men left and food supplies dangerously low, Burgoyne bowed to the inevitable. On October 17, 1777, he surrendered himself and his entire army to General Gates.

Today the British defeat at Saratoga is considered to be another of those "decisive battles of history," because it emboldened France to enter the war on the American side, thereby assuring eventual victory. But, as we shall see, the French were already sliding into the war, and, though the news of Saratoga may have hastened their decision, it did not determine it. What Burgoyne's disaster *did* accomplish was to convince the British that they dared not risk even large bodies of troops adrift in the American wilderness surrounded by an armed and hostile population. So during the entire critical winter of 1777–78, British forces remained locked up in Philadelphia, Newport, and New York. After Saratoga no British army ever again ventured more than fifty miles from the protecting guns and supply bases of the Royal Navy. While this spared English lives, it was no way to suppress a vast rebellion. Except in the seacoast cities, American loyalists could henceforth expect little help from the king's forces. In the interior loyalist influence steadily declined among the watchfully waiting majority of the population. The rebels, on the other hand, were left unmolested to consolidate their political power base. The radicalization of the American countryside proceeded apace.

All of which, of course, was not immediately perceptible to Washington and his ragged band at Valley Forge. A victory had been won, and that lifted their spirits for a while. But ahead lay the cruelest winter of the war . . .

## THE WAY IT WAS:
*"Lord—Lord—Lord!"*

*"Dec. 11th*—I am prodigious sick & cannot get anything comfortable—what in the name of Providence can I do with a fit of sickness in this place where nothing appears pleasing to the sicken'd eye & nauseating stomach. But I doubt not Providence will find a way out for my relief . . .

*"Dec. 12th*—A bridge of wagons made across the Schuyl-

kill last night, consisting of 36 wagons, with a bridge of rails between each. Some skirmishing down the river. Militia and dragoons brought into camp several prisoners. Sun set—We are ordered to march over the river—it snows—I'm sick—eat nothing—no whiskey—no baggage—Lord—Lord—Lord. The army were till sunrise crossing the river—some at the wagon bridge, & some at the raft bridge below. Cold & uncomfortable . . .

"*Dec. 14th*—Prisoners & deserters are continually coming in. The Army, who have been surprisingly healthy hitherto, now begin to grow very sickly from the continued fatigues they have suffered this campaign. Yet they still show spirit of alacrity & contentment not to be expected from so young troops. I am sick—discontented—and out of humor. Poor food—hard lodging—cold weather—fatigue—nasty clothes—nasty cookery—vomit half my time—smoked out of my senses—the Devil's in it—I can't endure it—why are we sent here to starve and freeze—what sweet felicities have I left at home—a charming wife—pretty children—good food—good cookery— all agreeable—all harmonious. Here, all confusion—smoke & cold—hunger & filthiness—a pox on my bad luck. Here comes a bowl of beef soup—full of burnt leaves and dirt, sickish enough to make a Hector spew—away with it Boys—I'll live like the chameleon upon air. . . .

"There comes a soldier—his bare feet are seen thro' his worn out shoes—his legs nearly naked from the tatt'red remains of an only pair of stockings—his breeches not sufficient to cover his nakedness—his shirt hanging in strings—his hair dishevell'd—his face meagre—his whole appearance pictures a person forsaken & discouraged. He comes and cries with an air of wretchedness & despair—I am sick—my feet lame—my legs are sore—my body cover'd with this tormenting itch—my clothes worn out—my constitution is broken—my former activity is exhausted by fatigue—hunger and cold—I fail fast, I shall soon be no more! And all the reward I shall get will be—'Poor Will is dead.' . . .

"*Dec. 21st*—Preparations made for huts. Provisions scarce. Mr. Willis went homeward—sent a letter to my wife. Heartily wish myself at home—my skin & eyes are almost spoil'd with continual smoke.

"A general cry thro' the camp this evening among the soldiers—'No meat! No meat!'—the distant vales echo'd back the melancholy sound—'No meat! No meat!' Imitating the noise of crows and owls also, made a part of the confused music.

"What have you for dinner, boys? 'Nothing but fire cake & water, Sir.' At night—'Gentlemen, the supper is ready.' What is your supper, lads? 'Fire cake & water, Sir.'

"*Dec. 22nd*—Lay excessive cold & uncomfortable last night—my eyes are started out of their orbits like a rabbit's eyes, occasion'd by a great cold—and smoke.

"What have you got for breakfast, lads? 'Fire cake and water, Sir.' . . .

"*Dec. 25th—Christmas*—We are still in tents—when we ought to be in huts—the poor sick, suffer much in tents this cold weather—But we now treat them differently from what they used to be at home . . . We give them mutton & grog . . . But very few of the sick men die . . .

"*Dec. 28th*—Yesterday, upwards of fifty officers in General Greene's Division resigned their commissions—six or seven of our regiment are going the like today. All this is occasion'd by officers' families being so much neglected at home on account of provisions. Their wages will not by considerable purchase a few trifling comfortables here in camp, & maintain their families at home, while such extravagant prices are demanded for the common necessaries of life . . .

"*1778, January 1st—New Year*. I am alive. I am well . . .

"*Jan. 3rd*—Our hut, or rather our hermit's cell, goes on briskly—having a short allowance of bread this morning, we divided it with great precision . . .

"*Sunday, Jan. 4th*— . . . I was called to relieve a soldier tho't to be dying—he expir'd before I reach'd the hut. He was an Indian—an excellent soldier—and an obedient good natur'd fellow. He engaged for money doubtless as others do—but he has serv'd his country faithfully—he has fought for those very people who disinherited his forefathers—having finished his pilgrimage, he was discharged from the War of Life & Death. His memory ought to be respected, more than those rich ones who supply the world with nothing better than money and vice. There the poor fellow lies, not superior to a clod of earth—his mouth wide open—his eyes staring. Was he affrighted at the scene of death—or the consequences of it?—doubtless both—but he has doubtless acted agreeable to the dictates of Nature in the course of his whole life—why should he then be afraid of the consequences of death? . . .

"*8th*—Unexpectedly got a furlough. Set out for home. The very worst of riding—mud & mire."

Albigence Waldo
Surgeon, Valley Forge

# 8 | The French Connection

*No doubt, if the Kings of France and Spain had martial ten-*
*dencies—if they obeyed the dictates of their own interests, and,*
*perhaps, the justice of their cause . . . they would doubtless*
*feel that Providence had evidently chosen that very hour for*
*humiliating England.*    –Charles Gravier, Comte de Vergennes

Since that black day in Paris in 1763 when France, humbled
by her loss of the Seven Years' War, had been forced to cede
an empire to Great Britain, thoughts of revenge had never been
far from the minds of her rulers. Indeed, the ink was hardly
dry on the treaties of peace when the Duc de Choiseul, head of
the French ministry, began preparing for yet another round in
the endless wars between England and France. He set about
reorganizing the French army, improving the state-owned
armaments industry, and strengthening the French alliance
with Spain. Of greater significance, he began the task of re-
building the French fleet into a real rival for the Royal Navy's
worldwide maritime supremacy. Nor did the canny Choiseul
overlook the possibility of stirring up trouble between Britain
and her colonies. He dispatched various agents to North
America who were to report upon the activities of American
rebels—especially such promising organizations as the Sons of
Liberty. But as the years dragged by with nothing decisive
happening in the colonies, Choiseul began to fear that British
luck would hold. "The English will never cut each other's
throats to the extent that we desire," he remarked sadly. The
Duc de Choiseul's appetite for vengeance proved too unsettling
to His Most Christian Majesty, Louis XV, king of France.

Choiseul was dismissed from the government in 1770. Upon his departure the Ministry of Foreign Affairs was placed in the hands of a far wilier and much more cautious diplomat, Charles Gravier, Comte de Vergennes.

Vergennes, though he too wished to humble British pride, realized that France was too weak to challenge British supremacy immediately. Since those glorious days when the armies of Louis XIV had dominated Europe, France had declined in power and prestige. In 1772, Poland, a French ally, was partitioned by Russia, Prussia, and Austria; in 1774, Turkey, another ally, was dismembered by Russia. In neither case could France do more than stand by helplessly and watch. Furthermore, the new king, Louis XVI, was unambitious, dull, and totally uninterested in the great European game of power politics. His favorite pastimes were repairing clocks and fretting over governmental expenses. Taught by his father that extravagance was the bane of the Bourbons and the cause of all the miseries to which French society was the heir, Louis XVI determined to cut expenses to the bone. Although he could do little to restrain the wild spending of his frivolous Austrian wife, Marie Antoinette, Louis realized that her extravagances would be as nothing compared to the costs of waging war—something he determined to avoid.

As for helping rebel republicans in North America—even at a distance of three thousand miles, their doctrines sounded entirely too sinister to Louis. The triumph of republican principles anywhere in the world would be a blow to the cause of monarchy. And that institution, especially in France, could not afford many more setbacks. Furthermore, there were those close to the king who predicted that a free America might one day become "a great military and naval power, and will be very ambitious, and so, terrible to Europe." Before pulling down the British Empire, Louis XVI wanted to be very sure he was not helping to establish an even more dangerous enemy to Europe and to monarchism.

In this respect, however, French opinion, even among the

aristocratic ruling class, was divided—the divisions reflecting those strains which were shortly to shatter the fabric of French society and bring on the Revolution of 1789. For in the last quarter of the eighteenth century France—royal, feudal France, still dominated by the *ancien régime*—was a social shell of seething discontent. All government was concentrated in the hands of a few great aristocrats faithful only to the king and their own pockets. The lesser nobility chafed away idle and frivolous days waiting upon the king at Versailles. Merchants and businessmen of the emerging middle classes found their ambitions thwarted and their business hamstrung by outmoded but rigid feudal rules and regulations. The urban poor, especially in Paris, lived on the edge of starvation with no social or political means to improve their lot. And beneath this entire superstructure there labored the vast mass of the sullen, ignorant, and feudally bound French peasantry. A single spark might ignite this social tinderbox at' any moment—and for years discontented French intellectuals had been trying to strike one.

For a generation French thinkers, poets, and writers had pointed to America as an example of what society might be. Such *philosophes* as Diderot found inspiration in Pennsylvania, where one could lead the good life without a nobility or an established church. Voltaire especially admired the Quakers, who evidently meant peace when they talked peace. Rousseau wrote of the North American Indians as "unspoiled children of nature," an example of how happy men might be freed from the trammels of society. Condorcet was so inspired by what he read of Connecticut that he signed one of his pamphlets "Un Bourgeois de New Haven." Du Pont de Nemours, whose descendants would one day establish an industrial empire in Delaware, declared Virginia to be an example of how all wealth was really derived from agriculture. Even Robert Turgot, Louis XVI's much hated minister of finance, wrote that Americans were "the hope of the world. They may become its model." But, of course, with the exception of Turgot, these men were enemies of the Bourbon monarchy and all that it stood for.

Why, then, with French society trembling on the brink of revolution, did the French ruling class ever agree to come to the aid of American republicans, the success of whose cause could only serve to further undermine their own position? Partly because of the old desire to humble mighty Britain. For, it was observed, "If the maritime power of England falls, France naturally and inevitably takes her place. By her position alone she inherits all that England loses." Partly, too, because a successful war against England might well unite French society and thereby strengthen the position of the monarchy as the symbol of French glory. But mainly, it must be confessed, the French ruling class determined to help the American rebels because "those whom the gods would destroy, they first make mad."

The French aristocracy had already been isolated, weakened, and blinded by its parasitic role as a frivolous, unnecessary burden upon the French nation. The alienation of the French ruling class from all contact with political reality had been going on for generations. Had that ruling class been at all capable of understanding the real meaning of republican success in North America, it would likewise have been capable of foreseeing and so, perhaps, of avoiding, its own bloody destruction in the approaching French Revolution of 1789—a revolution which would look to American success for much of its inspiration.

Vergennes's ambition, aside from teaching the English a lesson, did not aspire to the re-creation of a French empire. He did not want to take on the British imperial headache. Freedom of commerce with the Americans offered a better prospect of prosperity than did the recovery of Canada or Nova Scotia. A West Indian island or two might be helpful sources of revenue—but France's main benefits from a British defeat would be the restoration of her predominance on the European continent.

The realization that colonial rebellion was serious enough

to offer an opportunity for French intervention was impressed on Vergennes during the summer of 1775 by one of his foreign agents, a young playwright named Caron de Beaumarchais, author of the popular comedy, *The Barber of Seville*. Beaumarchais, stationed in London, had developed many contacts with English liberals and American rebels. He began bombarding Vergennes with reports of impending civil strife in England and of the grim determination which motivated the Americans. Helping those rebels, Beaumarchais insisted, would bring to Louis XVI a "harvest of glory and repose." Impressed, but far from convinced, Vergennes dispatched a secret agent to America in September 1775 to act as an observer. This officer, Achard de Bonvouloir, was to assure rebel leaders that France wished them well and harbored no intentions of reclaiming Canada. His instructions were, of course, oral—he was not to claim any official capacity or to commit the French government to anything whatsoever.

Meantime, the Continental Congress had already begun fishing for foreign aid. In November 1775 it appointed a Committee of Secret Correspondence to establish contact with potential supporters in England, Ireland, "and other parts of the world," meaning, of course, France. For colonial rebel leaders had always assumed that the French would be delighted to help them should their quarrel with England develop into outright war. Even before the British evacuation of Boston, Congress had already decided (on March 3, 1776) to send Silas Deane, a delegate from Connecticut, to negotiate for French help with Vergennes in Paris. But by that time Vergennes, through Beaumarchais, had already been in touch with Arthur Lee, Congress's agent in London, and had, furthermore, persuaded Louis XVI (against that monarch's better judgment) to supply arms and munitions to the rebels.

This could not, of course, be done openly—for that would have been an outright act of war against Great Britain, a step Vergennes was not yet prepared to take. But a scheme was devised which would, it was hoped, fool the English. Beaumarchais was secretly supplied with funds from the French Treasury and told to set up an export business which would be named Hortalez & Co. This company would purchase arms and munitions in France and dispatch them to the French West Indies. There American ships might pick them up and run the British blockade to deliver them at Boston or Charleston or wherever they could. Everything was to be kept as secret as possible, and even if the British did find out about the "private" activities of Hortalez & Co., they could not accuse the French government itself of gunrunning.

The disguise was a thin one; no one could purchase arms or munitions in France without the permission of the French government (from whom, in fact, the purchases had to be made). It would not be long before the British realized that "goods" shipped by Hortalez & Co. were not really destined for the West Indies. But the plan had the merit of providing the English with a means of saving face—they did not *have* to accuse the French government of outright intervention in their imperial affairs. Instead, they could simply complain of the laxity of French supervision of private commerce—an arguable matter which need not provoke war.

In any event, the British, through their own spies, knew all about Vergennes's plans and about the secret activities of Hortalez & Co. Even if they had not employed a first-rate intelligence service, the posturings and clownish playacting of Beaumarchais would have given the game away. For young Beaumarchais loved nothing better than playing spy. He was forever adopting outlandish disguises and swaggering around French ports from which "secret" shipments of arms were to be dispatched. He also enjoyed the role of "mystery man of great importance," and could never quite refrain from dropping boastful hints, especially to the ladies of his acquaintance, of his real mission. Unwilling, however, to add to its enemies, Lord North's government confined itself at first, as Vergennes had foreseen, to official complaints about Hortalez & Co., while relying upon the Royal Navy to intercept arms shipments bound for the colonies.

Silas Deane, who arrived in Paris in June 1776, was

joined six months later by Benjamin Franklin, who was without doubt the greatest ambassador ever sent from the New World to the Old. Already famous in France for his homely philosophy (his *Way to Wealth* had been translated as *La Science du Bonhomme Richard*) and for his scientific research and inventions (he was the first American ever to be elected to the French Academy of Sciences), Franklin played the part of simple, pure-spirited republican to perfection. His plain, homespun appearance charmed the glittering courtiers of Versailles, while his deep cunning was effectively disguised behind an aged, benign face adorned by a pair of innocent bifocal spectacles (one of his inventions) perched low on a huge, sympathetic nose. In a Paris filled with illusions about virtuous American "children of nature," Franklin was an instant success. He moved freely through every stratum of French society, mingling with the great and the unknown with equal ease. His gallantry to the ladies (especially those married to influential husbands) soon assumed scandalous proportions—but of this, too, his hosts approved.

Franklin's job was not simply to expedite the shipment of more French guns, munitions, and uniforms to the colonies, or to beg for more money and credit; Silas Deane and Arthur Lee were already doing that. It was to embroil France in total war with Great Britain. For by the end of 1776 it had become apparent to Congress that only outright French intervention could save the rebel cause. Vergennes, however, was not yet ready to take such a risk, and Franklin was much too wily a diplomat to push him. Instead, the good doctor devoted himself to disrupting Anglo-French relations through the "caught-in-the-act" method. His principal tools in this were American privateers.

Congress had originally assumed (correctly) that the building of an American navy would be a mere waste of effort in the face of Britain's tremendous naval ascendancy. Washington had, it was true, commissioned a few armed merchantmen at Boston, placing them under the command of one Ezek Hopkins. Hopkins raided Nassau in the Bahamas in March

1776, capturing much needed ammunition. This semi-private "navy" (of seven ships) soon evaporated, however. Congress then created an official navy and started to build ships for it. Almost all of these ships were either permanently blockaded in port or burned by British naval landing parties. But regular warships were not the only means of carrying on naval warfare in the eighteenth century. There was also privateering, a kind of legalized piracy whereby a government would issue "letters of marque" (commissions) to privately owned vessels authorizing them to raid an enemy's merchant shipping.

The lure of privateering lay in the handsome profits owners, captains, and crews made through the sale of captured goods and ships. Congress issued letters of marque with a liberal hand, and within a few months of the outbreak of hostilities around Boston, the Atlantic began to swarm with swift, determined Yankee privateers. Lightly gunned but too fast to be caught by Royal Navy frigates, these privateers soon raised havoc with British shipping, raiding even into the English Channel and the Irish Sea. They were hard to suppress at the source because the North American coastline abounded in small inlets and rivers where such ships could be built and from which they could sally forth on dark and blustery nights. The Royal Navy could not possibly blockade every mile of the American Atlantic coast.

But the privateers had problems too, the most important of which was what to do with captured merchantmen. If the privateers were to make money (the whole idea of the exercise), they had to sell captured vessels—but they could not run their prizes past the Royal Navy's blockade of American ports. Therefore captured British vessels were herded into French or Dutch ports for sale—to the grave and deepening displeasure of the British government. Not only did American privateers dispose of their captures in supposedly neutral continental ports—they also took on munitions and supplies there.

All of this was hazily legal according to what passed for international law in the eighteenth century—*provided one re-*

*garded the United Colonies as an independent nation.* Since France did not officially recognize American independence, however, the use of French ports by Yankee privateers was *totally* illegal, as the British Ambassador at Versailles continually reminded Vergennes. The French, however, as in the case of their "secret" shipments of supplies, pretended to be unaware of the activities of American privateers in their ports, and promised to "tighten" port controls. All of which presented Franklin with an obvious opportunity.

For while apparently doing everything he could to disguise the activities of Yankee sea raiders in French ports, Franklin from time to time "leaked" news of them to the British. This would produce a howl of anguish from His Majesty's Ambassador at Versailles, elicit more French equivocation, and thus snap yet another thread in the already frayed fabric of peace between the two countries. It was by official French response to this question of privateers (who struck Britain where it hurt most—in her commerce) and not by the activities of Hortalez & Co. that England judged French intentions. By the middle of 1777 damage inflicted on British commerce by American privateers had caused Lloyd's of London's maritime insurance rates to jump to a staggering 20 percent of ship-plus-cargo value—and Vergennes daily expected a British ultimatum on the subject.

But despite all this, Louis XVI was still king of France and, although he generally accepted Vergennes's advice, he would by no means engage in war against Britain without the help of his cousin, Charles III, Bourbon king of Spain. The so-called Family Compact between these two monarchs was the bedrock and anchor of Louis's foreign policy.

Spain, guided by her able foreign minister, Floridablanca, had an altogether different view of the American rebellion than did France. While the French, after 1763, had renounced imperial pretensions in the New World, Spain was still in possession of a very great transatlantic empire. This embraced all of South America (except Portuguese Brazil), all of Central

America, Mexico, and that huge area between the Mississippi River and the Pacific Ocean known as "Louisiana." These tremendous realms, from which Spain drew vast sums of treasure annually, were but thinly protected. Rebellion in the English colonies might well spark off rebellion in the Spanish. Furthermore, if the Americans succeeded in establishing a new nation, would they not turn greedy and aggressive eyes toward the Spanish dominions? And if Spain was dragged into a French war against England, with what could she defend her overseas possessions against the Royal Navy? True, Spain wanted to regain Gibraltar (ceded to Britain in 1763), and Vergennes was offering the return of the Floridas as well, but on balance Spanish interests demanded the preservation of peace with Britain—at least until such time as British defeat seemed certain.

Then, on December 3, 1777, news arrived in Paris of Burgoyne's disastrous defeat at Saratoga, and Benjamin Franklin prepared to make the most of it. He did not go about this by rushing to Vergennes with assurances that the capture of one small British army spelled the doom of the British Empire and the certain victory of the Americans. On the contrary, he used the victory at Saratoga to enter into negotiations with English representatives in Paris. These agents, dispatched by Lord North some weeks previously, were instructed by the British government (chastened by Saratoga) to offer the Americans the most generous and liberal terms. Everything the rebels had been demanding for years, including complete home-rule government, would be granted them, provided only that they agreed to remain within the British Empire. And to prove his sincerity, Lord North introduced a bill into Parliament in November 1777 embodying these terms. Franklin, of course, had no intention of settling for anything less than complete independence—but he was able to use these negotiations to play on Vergennes's fear that the colonies might, after all, return to the British fold.

The trick worked. Seeing France's great opportunity to

strike down British pretensions slipping away, as he thought, Vergennes hurried to the king to insist on action with or without Spain's agreement. Louis was persuaded, and on February 6, 1778, Vergennes signed two treaties with the American representatives—one of friendship and commerce, the other of alliance. Furthermore, the alarmed Vergennes allowed Franklin to write his own terms—which consequently greatly favored the Americans. The French agreed that neither nation would make peace with Britain until she recognized American independence; that France would relinquish all claims on her previous North American possessions and would favor an American annexation of Canada; and that each party was to judge for itself what military efforts it ought to undertake. In return for this, the Americans would recognize any French conquests among the British West Indian islands (but not the Bermudas) and agreed not to make a separate peace with England.

A secret article provided for Spain's eventual adherence to the treaty, but this was not to be forthcoming until France formally bound herself to help the Spaniards reconquer Gibraltar. Floridablanca reluctantly led his country into the war in June 1779, but Spanish help to the Americans was limited to small-scale financial assistance, while Spanish military activity was restricted to the occupation of the Floridas. Thus, at a stroke of the pen, Vergennes and Franklin transformed a minor colonial rebellion into a full-scale European war.

It almost became a world war—largely through the activities of one of those pestiferous American privateers. Its name lost to history, one of these raiders in July 1778 destroyed eight British merchantmen carrying neutral goods to Archangel in Russia. This prompted the Russian empress, Catherine II, to propose to various European powers the creation of a "League of Armed Neutrality," which would enforce the protection of neutral commerce at sea against both Yankee privateers and British blockading fleets. Eventually, Denmark, Prussia, Sweden, a brace of petty Italian states, and Holland joined this league—without major consequences for anyone at all except the unfortunate Dutch, who thereby became themselves embroiled in war with England in December 1780.

News of the French alliance reached Congress in May 1778—just in time to stiffen congressional resolve not to accept Lord North's conciliatory proposals. The British mission which had come to negotiate was allowed to cool its heels in New York. Meantime, American rebels from Boston to Savannah toasted His Most Christian Majesty, Louis XVI of France, and congratulated each other that victory was now assured. It was —but it would be many years in coming.

## THE WAY IT WAS:

*"How will it sound in history?"*

"As an American citizen, I rejoice in the prospect of so speedy and, I hope, an effectual aid. But *as a soldier,* I am dissatisfied. How will it sound in history, that the United States of America could not, or rather, would not, make an exertion, when the means were amply in their power, which might at once rid them of their enemies, and put them in possession of that liberty and safety for which we have been so long contending. By Heavens! if our rulers had any modesty, they would blush at the idea of calling in foreign aid! 'tis really abominable, that we should send to France *for soldiers,* when there are so many sons of America idle. Such a step ought not (had these great men any sensibility) to have been taken until the strength of the country had been nearly exhausted, and our freedom tottering on the brink of ruin. Let us be indebted to France, Spain or even the Devil himself, if he could furnish it, for a navy, because we cannot get one seasonably among ourselves. But do let us, unless we are contented to be transmitted to posterity with disgrace, make an exertion of our own strength by land, and not owe our independence entirely to our allies."

Major Samuel Shaw
Valley Forge

# 9 | "The Congress Are Fallen into General Contempt"

*The people are a mighty ocean—and we are the fish who swim in this sea.*
                                              —Mao Tse-tung

. *We are daily and hourly oppressing the people—souring their tempers—and alienating their affections.*   —George Washington

When, on May 6, 1778, General Washington officially announced the Franco-American alliance to the Continental Army at Valley Forge, the troops, after shouting hurrahs and (we are told) such improbable mouth-filling slogans as "Long live the friendly European powers!," put on a parade. The remarkable thing about this parade was that the men marched in step, to the beat of their drums, held their muskets properly, did not trip over themselves, and maintained their formations.

That the army had finally learned these rudimentary military skills was due to the tireless activity of a Prussian aristocrat, General Baron von Steuben, a fine drillmaster and a mighty liar. The lies were harmless enough—the baron passed himself off to Congress as, variously, a lieutenant general, a quartermaster general, and an aide-de-camp of Frederick the Great himself. He was none of these things, but he was an able officer of the Prussian army—and he was a genuine volunteer in the American cause, asking no rewards until and unless he proved his worth. Congress made him a general and sent him to Valley Forge. There he encountered the ragged, half-starved, huddled mob that Washington called an army and within a few months transformed it into a trained military force.

If the absolute necessity for precision marching and disciplined drill which all eighteenth-century armies required seems to us somehow irrelevant to actual fighting, this is only because weapons, which determine tactics, have changed. The eighteenth-century soldier was armed with a weapon (whether musket or rifle) which took about half a minute to load, aim, and fire—and was not accurate for much more than a hundred yards. The decisive instrument of death on a battlefield was the bayonet, not the bullet. Eighteenth-century soldiers, like the ancient warriors of Philip of Macedon, were really spear carriers, and the art of using them effectively in battle was that of organizing and hurling masses of these spear carriers at the enemy.

To maneuver these masses in such a way that they enjoyed, at the point of contact, numerical superiority, surprise, or an advantage in terrain was the key to victory. When it is remembered that this maneuvering had to be done under fire in the face of the enemy, it will be understood that the men had to be trained to execute complicated movements with instantaneous precision. The lack of such training had cost the Americans bloody defeats on Long Island and Manhattan and had reduced Washington to fighting a guerrilla war. But ambushes, sniping, and hit-and-run raids would never defeat a British army in open, face-to-face combat—and someday, somewhere, the Americans were going to have to do that.

Steuben, a hard-driving taskmaster who spoke a broken but useful English—interlaced with earsplitting "God damns!" —soon made himself popular with the rank and file. He understood at once that Americans were not Prussians and could not be subjected to Prussian discipline. In the Prussian army, "officers say to a soldier, 'Do this,' and he does it," Steuben observed, "but I, I am obliged to say, 'This is the reason why you ought to do that,' and then he does it." Steuben taught the men to wield their bayonets, to march properly, to execute battlefield maneuvers, and to advance to the charge. He also composed a manual of arms, elements of which survive to this day in American military training.

The baron was by no means the only European officer.

who served with the Americans. Benjamin Franklin was besieged in Paris by hundreds of unemployed officer-veterans, mostly soldiers of fortune who expected high rank and even higher pay for their services. Many proved perfectly worthless, but some, like Steuben, were invaluable.

Among these was the Marquis de Lafayette, a young (he was nineteen when he reached America) and wealthy minor French aristocrat whose head was full of fashionable ideals about liberty and glory. He arrived in 1777 in a ship equipped at his own expense, and Congress immediately made him a major general in the Continental Army. Modest, hard-working, and handsome, Lafayette made an instant hit with officers and men (for whom he bought food and clothing with his own money). He especially charmed Washington, who eventually gave him a small independent command. He proved a brave and capable officer—and his connections at the French court were one day going to prove decisive.

And there were others. There was the Chevalier Duportail, a French engineering officer who designed many forts and other defensive works for Washington; there was Thaddeus Kosciuszko, a Polish officer who planned the first fortifications at West Point; there was Casimir Pulaski, a Polish cavalryman who would die at the head of his troops charging the British fortifications outside Savannah; and there was the self-styled Baron de Kalb, a tough German soldier of fortune who would die at the battle of Camden. These men, and others who never achieved their fame, were sincere adherents of the self-proclaimed ideals of the American rebellion. They may be compared in our times, not to the mercenaries employed on either side in recent national liberation wars, but rather to the international volunteers who fought against fascism in Spain from 1936 to 1939. Those who survived to return to their homelands (like Lafayette and Kosciuszko) often became heroes of later revolutions and uprisings.

While the newly trained Continental Army was greeting the news from Paris with parades and hurrahs, Lord North and his colleagues in London tried to fathom French intentions. With her rebuilt, again powerful navy, France had the capability of striking hard—but where would the blow fall? The Royal Navy was not equal to the task of defending against a possible French invasion of England, a possible French assault on the British West Indies, and a possible French intervention in North America all at the same time. But one tempting target for French attack—Sir William Howe's forces in Philadelphia—could, at least, be removed. Accordingly, Howe was relieved of his command, and his army, now headed by cautious General Sir Henry Clinton, was ordered to evacuate the rebel capital and hole up in New York City, where it could better defend itself against a French fleet.

That fleet was on its way. Taking the advice of an American sea raider named John Paul Jones, the French Admiralty had ordered a powerful squadron under the command of Admiral Comte d'Estaing to proceed to the mouth of the Delaware. There it was to cooperate with the Continental Army in bottling up the British. But bureaucratic delay and foul weather intervened. By the time d'Estaing's ships arrived (July 8, 1778), the British had escaped. The French fleet followed them to New York, but not liking the grim look of a British squadron cleared for action in the Narrows, d'Estaing headed for Newport, Rhode Island. There his projected landing was baffled by a storm, and his ships were forced to seek refuge in Boston—where his sailors on shore leave were promptly beaten up by Sam Adams's waterfront toughs. Finally, a few weeks later, d'Estaing set sail for the happier campaigning waters of the West Indies—and so ended the first attempt at Franco-American combined operations.

When the British evacuated Philadelphia, Washington perceived an opportunity to strike. He now commanded some 24,000 men against 13,000 regulars under Sir Henry Clinton. Furthermore, the British, as they marched across New Jersey on their way north, were encumbered by their usual heavy baggage train—their march averaged no more than six miles a day. Accordingly, the Continentals tried to intercept them at Monmouth Courthouse on June 28, 1778. Tried, but owing to the bungling and cowardice of American general Charles Lee (for which he was later court-martialed and dismissed), failed. The British regulars drove their badly mishandled foes from the field and continued their march undisturbed, arriving in New York with bag and baggage a few days later.

Washington posted his army at White Plains, north of the city, to prevent any British march up the Hudson Valley or into New England. So long as the waters around the New York islands were dominated by the Royal Navy, no attack on Clinton's forces there was possible. For his part, Sir Henry had no plans of an aggressive nature; he was content to enjoy the hospitality of the city. Although neither Clinton nor Washington could have foreseen the fact, large-scale military operations in the northern and middle colonies were now at an end. Aside from small-scale raids and hit-and-run expeditions, their two armies would never again meet on the battlefield.

But the political war continued—and despite the French alliance, the rebel cause looked more and more hopeless as time wore on. Take, for example, the activities of the American loyalists.

The loyalist party persisted in every part of America throughout the entire course of the war. Although including former royal officeholders, wealthy merchants, New York patroons, and the Anglican clergy, the loyalists were drawn from every rank and stratum of American society. Most of them were farmers, artisans, small shopkeepers, and frontiersmen— and their attachment to the British cause was sincere. Families everywhere were divided; such leading American rebels as John Adams, Otis, Lee, Franklin, Washington, Jefferson, and Randolph numbered loyalists among their kinsmen. Along the southern frontier there is little doubt that the loyalists formed a majority, but everywhere they were an important minority. Numbers varied from state to state—perhaps as many as 50 percent in New York, as few as 8 percent in Connecticut.

Significantly, wherever a British army held firm, loyalists flocked to its protection and offered their services. When the British army evacuated Philadelphia, more than three thousand loyalists left with them. Once ensconced in New York, Sir Henry Clinton began enrolling special loyalist fighting units. New York eventually provided more troops for the king than for Congress. Loyalist battalions such as the Rangers and the Loyal Greens waged the bitterest kind of war against the rebels. When loyalist and rebel Americans met in battle, no quarter was given or asked; the wounded were often massacred and prisoners were generally hanged. Thus the American rebellion developed, in many areas, into civil war.

A further inflammation of the hatred between rebels and loyalists was the use made by each side of Indians. The wooing of the tribes had begun as early as 1775, when Congress sent agents to the frontier to seek alliances with the various nations. But Congress's efforts in this direction were handicapped by one very painfully obvious fact; the victory of the rebels must spell the doom of the Indians. Throughout the war the policy of frontier Americans was what it had always been and was always to be—genocide against the Indian race. The Indians were aware that among the cause of the rebellion had been the king's Proclamation of 1763, which protected them in their lands, and they knew what to expect at the hands of an independent American nation.

In any competition for Indian support, the British held all the advantages. Not only were they the self-proclaimed protectors of Indian lands, they were also much better prepared to supply the tribes with guns, powder, and liquor. Indian captains in His Majesty's service were clad in resplendent uniforms, the few in American service often went naked. The most important of all the tribes, the mighty Iroquois nation, remained loyal to its hundred-year-old friendship with Great Britain. Led by the American loyalist colonel Walter Butler, the Iroquois (and their comrades, the loyalist Rangers) went on a killing spree in 1778. Thousands of frontier families in the old northwest were butchered, and garrisons of Continental troops were massacred after they surrendered. Entire districts were depopulated, and the western frontier was pushed all the way back to Schenectady, New York. The work of a generation of settlement was undone. This kind of bloody frontier fighting spared no one—including, eventually, Colonel Butler himself, whose scalp decorated American headquarters for several days.

The key to the west, and thus of control of the Indian tribes, was the British fort at Niagara. It commanded the communications of a huge area extending west beyond Detroit and south through the Ohio Valley to the Pennsylvania frontier. A rebel attempt to capture the post in 1779, led by General John Sullivan, failed to come within a hundred miles of its objective. Throughout the war the west remained British, and as late as 1782, Indians were terrorizing the frontier.

Yet another source of manpower for which British and Americans competed was that of the black slaves. Here, again, the rebels were handicapped by the obvious fact that their success would only mean continued slavery for black men. With the British there was at least a chance for freedom. In writing the Declaration of Independence, Jefferson had included a harsh indictment of George III for supporting the slave trade. But at the insistence of delegates from the Carolinas and Georgia this paragraph was dropped from the final text. The planters of the deep south (in Virginia a changing economy made black slavery appear less and less profitable) could not bring themselves to condemn the king for what they considered to be a positive good.

But by 1778 the necessities of war were breaking down former prejudices. The fact was that very few white Americans wanted to join the Continental Army or even the various state militias. The manpower problem became critical. One way for a white man to avoid military service was to send a substitute—and for white men who owned black slaves, this was the easy way out. An increasing number of blacks joined the Continental ranks until, by 1778, there were an average of fifty blacks in every Continental regiment (nearly 1,000 blacks fought at Monmouth Courthouse). Not all of these were slave substitutes. The New England colonies, especially Massachusetts, had been enlisting free blacks since Bunker Hill—to the scandal and mortification of their southern brethren. But this was not necessarily a sign of moral superiority in the north.

The truth was that in the northern colonies, with their small-farm, artisan, and seafaring economies, black slavery was far from profitable and had never been widespread. True, the merchants and shipping magnates of Boston, New London, and New York made tremendous profits from the slave *trade*—but the British blockade had put an end to that. With no deeply rooted economic interest in slavery, northerners were more easily persuaded of the institution's moral evil than were southerners, whose entire plantation economy rested upon the backs of their black slaves. Reformers were therefore able to push emancipation laws through the rebel legislatures of Vermont, New Hampshire, Massachusetts, Pennsylvania, Rhode Island, and Connecticut during the war.

By 1779, Congress, which had maintained a discreet silence on the matter out of deference to southern delegates, was forced by the manpower crunch to offer black slaves their freedom if they would enlist for three years in the Continental Army. And when the British invaded the southern colonies later that same year, Congress recommended the immediate enlistment of five thousand black slaves in the Carolinas and Georgia. Yet so fearful were white slaveowners of arming the blacks that it soon became apparent that the southern plantation masters would prefer to lose the war rather than accept Congress's suggestion. But, again, political morality followed economic interest; for in Maryland and Virginia (where slavery was no longer essential to the economy and would not again become so until the invention of the cotton gin), slaves *were* enlisted. Maryland raised 750 blacks to fight in white regiments, while Virginia granted freedom to all who would serve in her militia. Of course, in these cases the slaveowners were always compensated by large cash payments for the loss of their "property."

Recognizing that slavery was where the rebellion in the south was most vulnerable, the British early in the war had offered freedom to all black slaves who would volunteer to serve with their forces. While slavery was the cruel basis of British West Indian prosperity and the slave trade a vital part of the British maritime economy, the institution of slavery was absolutely forbidden in the British Isles. British officers therefore took great pleasure in flinging in rebel faces Dr. Samuel Johnson's sarcastic question: "How is it that we hear the loudest yelps for liberty from the drivers of negroes?" And they took equal pleasure in stealing slaves from American masters and then selling them into a far worse bondage in the West Indies.

In 1781, Lord Cornwallis raided Jefferson's plantation at Monticello and carried off about thirty slaves. "Had this been done to give them freedom," Jefferson observed, "he would have done right." During the war many thousands of black slaves escaped from their American masters whenever a British army appeared in their neighborhood. To their credit, the British kept their promise of freedom to all blacks who would serve. When His Majesty's forces finally evacuated the southern port cities, an estimated 30,000 black freemen left with them. Why, then, did any blacks at all fight alongside the Continental forces? Almost always it was either to gain their personal freedom or because they were forced to do so by their masters. Like the Indians, black Americans had few illusions about their future in a racist culture.

If most Americans refused to fight in the rebel cause, few also could be found who were willing to support the struggle with their worldly goods. All through the war the Continental Army and state militias lacked food, clothing, arms, and transport. For weeks on end Washington's troops subsisted on hardtack and water. For years (until French supplies reached them) they went barefoot and nearly naked through the bitter cold of winter and the blistering heat of summer. And all of this was not due to any lack of food and clothing in the colonies. It was due to the indifference and greed of the overwhelming majority of their fellow countrymen. During the bitter winter of 1777–78, while the ragged Continentals starved and froze to death at Valley Forge, just a few miles away civilians were busily selling food and supplies of all kinds to the British army in Philadelphia. And this phenomenon of Americans profitably supplying their supposed enemies while resolutely ignoring the plight of their own soldiers appeared at all places and at all times throughout the war.

One cause of this was, of course, the lack of money. Congress could collect no taxes and was dependent upon the bounty of the individual states for funds. When that bounty proved insufficient (as it did from the very beginning), Congress resorted to the printing of paper money and IOUs. But these rapidly fell in value—both because Congress had no gold or silver with which to back its currency and because, as the war dragged on, it became less and less likely that the rebel cause would succeed. A British victory would make all Continental money worthless. Not only could Congress not pay for supplies. It could not pay its troops, either—except in dollars which had fallen to a value of less than one cent by 1780.

Maddened by poverty and suffering (while all around them they could see civilian profiteering), Continental troops took to foraging for supplies in the countryside. It was all they could do to survive. In 1780 the Pennsylvania Line fell upon their fat civilian compatriots with a fury which General Nathanael Greene declared was equal to the worst atrocities of the Hessians. Plundering troops were severely punished—but that did not solve the basic problem. Later in 1780 and in 1781 both the Pennsylvania and the New Jersey troops mutinied, their uprising being finally suppressed only by promises of better treatment and the hanging of a couple of ringleaders.

In desperation Congress tossed the problem back to the states. Unable to finance the rebellion, in 1780 it adopted the policy of asking each state to send a quota of food, clothing, munitions, and other material to the army directly. But this policy of "requisitions" brought little relief. The states were as unwilling or unable to supply real goods as they were to contribute paper money. Nor did Congress provide any means of transporting supplies to the army encampments. In the end Washington, to his great disgust, was forced to authorize army foraging (plundering) expeditions into the countryside or see his army melt away for want of provisions—and this further alienated civilian support.

Which provides us with an important clue as to what was really going on. When, more than one hundred and fifty years after the American rebellion, Mao Tse-tung wrote of his own ragged forces, "The people are a mighty ocean—and we are the fish who swim in this sea," he was summing up the central secret of every successful revolution. This principle is that revolutionary forces can survive only through the active help and cooperation of the masses of their fellow countrymen. Which is to say that a very great majority of the people must accept and support a revolution if it is to succeed. It cannot be won by a handful of conspirators or even by regiments or divisions of isolated "freedom fighters." The revolutionary army must express the will of a revolutionary people, must embody their hopes and emerge from their sufferings. For in the beginning, at least, established authority will always be better armed, better organized, and better supplied than rebel forces. To hide from the vengeance of this governing authority and to recruit new volunteers, rebel forces must submerge themselves in the vast sea of the people—and this they can never do if that sea is a hostile environment.

While it would be going too far to describe the American people as a hostile environment for the Continental Congress and Army, it was certainly an *indifferent* environment in most places and at most times. But this becomes understandable when we recall that the Americans were not engaged in making a revolution—despite all the social upheaval that accompanied the war. Here was no mass rising of a suppressed portion of the population seeking to wrest economic, social, and political state power from an oppressive establishment. Here was a struggle initiated and carried forward by the establishment itself—*against the pretensions of a rival establishment.*

Basically, the contest was to determine just who would henceforth profit from the exploitation of the vast, untapped wealth of North America—the English or the American ruling classes? It is no wonder, then, that the majority of Americans (like the majority of their English cousins) remained passive spectators of the struggle, except in those regions such as Boston, New Jersey, or the Vermont–New York wilderness, where the existence of a British army spelled immediate personal ruin.

In this sea of American indifference, Washington and Congress could barely keep their rebellion alive—despite all the propaganda and promises with which they filled the air. A kind of isolated, hit-and-run warfare was all that was possible to the Continental Army under these circumstances. And even that kind of fighting remained on so small a scale as to promise no prospect of eventual success. Although geography and the lack of speedy transport and communications made the British task of subduing rebellion extremely difficult, by 1779 it seemed they might succeed through rebel default—barring some outside calamity. But that calamity, in the shape of a French fleet and French armies on American soil, was about to descend.

### THE WAY IT WAS:

*"Treason! Treason! Treason! Black as Hell!"*

"Treason of the blackest dye was yesterday discovered. General Arnold, who commanded at West Point, lost to every sentiment of honor, of public and private obligation, was about to deliver up that important fort into the hands of the enemy. Such an event must have given the American cause a deadly wound if not a fatal stab. Happily the scheme was timely discovered to prevent the fatal misfortune. The providential train of circumstances which led to it, affords the most convincing proofs that the liberties of America are the object of divine protection. At the same time the treason is so regretted, the General cannot help congratulating the army on the happy discovery.

"Our enemies, despairing of carrying their point by force, are practicing every base art to effect, by bribery and corruption, what they cannot accomplish in a manly way. Great honor is due to the American army, that this is the first instance of treason of this kind, where many were to be expected from the nature of the dispute, and nothing is so high an ornament to the characters of the American soldiers as their withstanding all the arts and seductions of an insidious enemy.

"Arnold the traitor, has made his escape to the enemy, but Mr. André, Adjutant-General to the British Army, who came out as a spy to negotiate the business, is our prisoner.

"His Excellency the Commander-in-chief has arrived at West Point, from Hartford, and is now doubtless taking proper steps to unravel fully so hellish a plot."

> General Nathanael Greene
> Order of the Day,
> September 26, 1780

"Treason! Treason! Treason! Black as Hell! That a man so high on the lists of fame should be guilty as Arnold, must be attributed not only to original sin, but actual transgressions. Heaven and earth! we are all astonishment—each peeping at his next neighbor to see if any treason was hanging about him; nay, we even descended to a critical examination of ourselves.

"This surprise soon settled down into a fixed detestation and abhorrence of Arnold, which can receive no addition. His treason has unmasked him, the eeriest villain of centuries past, and set him in true colors. His conduct and sufferings at the northward has, in the eyes of the army and his country, covered a series of base, grovelling, dirty, scandalous, and rascally peculations and fraud . . .

". . . Avarice, cursed avarice, with unbounded ambition, void of every principle of honor, honesty, generosity or gratitude, induced the caitiff to make the first overtures to the enemy."

Colonel Alexander Scammel
Continental Army

# 10 | "O God! It Is All Over!"

*The war is not even entertaining–nothing but miscarriages and drawn battles. I believe the expense of the sum total will be the only striking event.*                          –Horace Walpole

A year and a half had passed since the conclusion of the Franco-American alliance—and neither ally had much to show for it. Washington's miserable army still watched and waited at White Plains while Sir Henry Clinton's forces enjoyed the hospitality of New York City. The war was at stalemate. It was at stalemate as far as the Americans were concerned because without sea power they could never eject the British from New York. And as far as Sir Henry was concerned, he dared not march into the interior beyond his naval line of supply and communications. So both sides engaged in meaningless raids which, while they had no effect on the outcome of the war, aroused bitterness and hatred.

Under instructions from the War Office to hit American seaports, Sir Henry dispatched small expeditionary forces up and down the coast. In 1778 these commando-type raids burned Egg Harbor in New Jersey, New Bedford and Fairhaven in Massachusetts, and Vineyard Haven on Martha's Vineyard. In 1779 a British expedition under Sir George Collier ravaged the towns around Chesapeake Bay, then returned to New York and, sailing up the Hudson, seized the American observation post at Stony Point. Frustrated by local militia from landing at New Haven, Connecticut (where they planned to burn Yale College), Sir Henry's men satisfied themselves with destroying Fairfield and Norwalk. None of these missions had any military value—their purpose was to terrify the rebels, who, as Sir Henry hoped, "are recovered from the phrensy which has distracted this unhappy country," and ought to "blush at their delusions." Far from blushing, Congress was enraged. It discussed a plan whereby Benjamin Franklin was to hire a gang of arsonists to burn London, beginning with Buckingham Palace. This scheme came to naught, but retaliation was on its way—to be administered by an American Scots immigrant sea raider named John Paul Jones.

That daring officer, in the little sloop of war *Ranger,* boldly sailed into the English port of Whitehaven, where he burned the shipping. When H.M.S. *Drake* attempted to intervene, Jones disabled and captured her. Encouraged by this success, Franklin and the French Admiralty in 1779 gave Jones command of a small task force consisting of an old armed merchant ship which, in honor of Franklin, Jones renamed *Bonhomme Richard,* a new frigate, *Alliance,* and three French ships—all under the American flag. With this force Jones boldly sailed completely around the British Isles, scaring the daylights out of Edinburgh and Newcastle. Then, on September 23, 1779, in the North Sea, he fell in with H.M.S. *Serapis,* a heavily armed frigate. Abandoned by the rest of his ships, Jones fought broadside to broadside against this formidable foe until *Bonhomme Richard* was a sinking ruin. When asked by the English captain whether he had struck his flag, Jones replied: "I have not yet begun to fight!" and led a wild mass of cutlass-swinging seamen onto *Serapis*'s deck. There, after a bitter fight, he received the English captain's surrender. *Bonhomme Richard* promptly sank, but Jones sailed *Serapis* into the neutral Dutch harbor of Texel, after winning the sea fight which has immortalized his name.

While his men kept themselves occupied by burning helpless villages on the seacoast, Sir Henry Clinton's thoughts turned to the south. In November 1778 a British expedition

from New York, under the command of Sir Archibald Camp-
bell, had captured Savannah, Georgia, with remarkable ease
and then advanced inland against light opposition. By the
spring of 1779, with American loyalists flocking to Sir Archibald's standard, a royal governor had been reinstated and a
loyalist assembly was meeting. At very little cost the colony of
Georgia was once more part of the empire. Ruminating on this
success, Sir Henry (and his superiors in London) were inclined
to ascribe it to the fact that a very large percentage of southern
Americans must be loyal to the crown in their hearts. In the
south His Majesty's forces might, at last, encounter that true
"land of Tories" they had been vainly seeking since 1776. And,
having reconquered the Carolinas and Virginia, British forces
could then roll north and so stamp out the remnants of rebellion. Sir Henry was urged forward in this enterprise by an able
and ambitious fellow officer, General Charles Lord Cornwallis.

Accordingly, in the spring of 1780, a large British expeditionary force sailed from New York under the command of
Clinton and Cornwallis. It included some 8,500 men (about
one-third of them American loyalists) embarked in ninety
transports and convoyed by fourteen men-of-war. On April 8
this formidable armada appeared off Charleston, South Carolina. To defend this city, rebel general Benjamin Lincoln (who
had originally been sent south by Washington to recapture
Savannah but failed) could muster only 1,200 Continentals (of
the South Carolina and Virginia lines), and about 2,000 local
militia. The British warships crashed through the fire of Fort
Moultrie and anchored off the city while Clinton and Cornwallis landed their regulars south of Charleston to invest the
place from the rear. On May 12 the rebels surrendered and the
British marched in—the greatest American defeat of the entire
war. Clinton set up a loyalist government in Charleston and
then sailed back to New York, leaving Cornwallis in command.

Using mainly his American loyalist troops, especially
Colonel Banastre Tarleton's Legion, Cornwallis overran almost
all of South Carolina within three months. The local rebel mili-

tia forces under General Thomas Sumter were overwhelmed. Cornwallis established fortified posts at Camden and Ninety Six to protect himself from attack from the north and placed strong garrisons in Savannah, Port Royal, and Charleston to protect the coast. The former royal governor now returned, and to all intents and purposes South Carolina, like Georgia, was back again in the empire.

In the meantime, in April 1780, when Clinton sailed south from New York, Washington, aware of his destination, had dispatched the Maryland and Delaware Line regiments from the Continental Army under General de Kalb to rescue the Carolinas. These veteran soldiers, exhausted and near starvation after an incredibly hard march, reached Hillsboro, North Carolina, on June 22. The states through which they had tramped failed to furnish them with supplies of any kind. They had to subsist on wild berries, green peaches, and green corn —but their sufferings were far from over. For by this time Congress had learned of the fall of Charleston and had appointed General Horatio Gates, the "hero of Saratoga," to supersede de Kalb in command.

What Congress did not know, but what any Continental soldier from Washington to the lowliest private could have told them (and did), was that Gates was not the hero of Saratoga— Benedict Arnold was. Gates nearly fumbled the Saratoga campaign away and then "forgot" to mention in his report Arnold's daring translation of defeat into victory—which may have started the vain and ambitious Arnold to thinking about which side would better appreciate his abilities. In any event, Gates took command from de Kalb in July and then marched his already exhausted troops through the pine wilderness to attack the British post at Camden. On August 16, 1780, Cornwallis fell upon Gates' famished army outside Camden and killed or captured almost all of it. De Kalb fell, mortally wounded, while Gates galloped away from the battlefield, and so out of the war. North Carolina now lay open and unprotected against Cornwallis's veterans.

The state had not long to wait. In September, following the victory at Camden, Cornwallis invaded North Carolina with his regulars and a separate column of some 1,500 American loyalist volunteers under the command of Major Patrick Ferguson. Ferguson's loyalists were looking for vengeance. They sent word ahead that they intended to burn rebel settlements and hang every rebel leader in North Carolina. This was a mistake, for it aroused the entire countryside against them. The informal North Carolina militia units were joined by rifle-toting frontiersmen from western Virginia, and on October 7, 1780, they caught Ferguson's force at King's Mountain. By day's end Ferguson was dead and every man of his command killed or captured.

This setback forced Cornwallis to retreat back to Winnsboro, South Carolina, where he remained all winter while his cavalry, commanded by Tarleton, skirmished with local partisan forces led by Pickens, Sumter, and Marion, the "Swamp Fox." All in all, the British strategy had been sound. Two colonies had been reconquered at little cost, and there *had* been a large outpouring of loyalist volunteers—Ferguson had recruited 4,000 in South Carolina in a matter of weeks. Come spring Cornwallis would conquer North Carolina and then move up into Virginia. Little resistance was expected.

Meantime Congress finally allowed Washington to appoint his own choice to command in the southern theater. He picked General Nathanael Greene, gave him 1,100 Continentals, and sent him to Charlotte, North Carolina. "The appearance of the troops," wrote Greene in January 1781, "was wretched beyond description, and their distress, on account of lack of provisions, was little less than their suffering for want of clothing and other necessities."

The same grim old story—an army without popular support, starving in the midst of plenty. But by now Congress had reached the conclusion that unless they did something about logistics, the war was as good as lost. Having failed to arouse the people to sacrifices on behalf of the cause, their credit exhausted both at home and abroad (Vergennes was warning Franklin that the French Treasury did, after all, have a bottom), the politicians in Congress now turned to the only solution still politically available to them. They entrusted the matter of finances and supply to a private merchant named Robert Morris. Of all the businessmen who had grown rich from the war, he had grown richest—therefore he presumably knew the secret of economic management. He was appointed superintendent of finance in January 1781, with sweeping powers over Continental resources, of which there were almost none.

Morris didn't want the job. He believed (correctly) that public office would expose him to "the envy and jealousy of mankind. . . . My opinion of mankind has grown worse from my experience of them." But if the rebel cause failed, so would Willing, Morris & Co., and conditions had now reached the point where it was, perhaps, time for a businessman to step in and "clean up the mess" in Philadelphia. In any event, he shouldered the burden, and his success was remarkable. It was remarkable chiefly because everyone knew that he was the richest man in America. Wealthy merchants knew that if Congress did not repay them, Morris would—and so did the French.

By dint of begging and borrowing on his personal credit, Morris was able to furnish enough supplies to see the Continental Army through the rest of the war. Once, when the troops refused to march without pay, Morris borrowed $20,000 from French General Rochambeau and another $20,000 from friends in Philadelphia to meet the soldiers' demands. Thus a miracle came to pass; on September 8, 1781, a major in the Continental Army confided to his diary: "This day will be famous in the Annals of History for being the first on which the Troops of the United States received one Month's Pay in Specie [coin]." From the various states Morris continued to receive nothing—except pleas for money. But through his exertions the Continental Army and, hence, the rebel cause were kept alive—which was in itself a very clear comment on the nature of the struggle.

While Morris undertook the appalling task of bringing American finances into order, Nathanael Greene led his little army (reinforced now by "Light-Horse" Harry Lee's cavalry) on the road back into South Carolina. On January 17, 1781, he routed Tarleton's loyalists at Cowpens near the old battlefield of King's Mountain, and on March 15 fought it out with Cornwallis's regulars at Guilford Courthouse. There, in one of the war's bloodiest battles, the British won—but at the staggering loss of more than 30 percent killed and wounded. With such losses, and having outrun his supplies, Cornwallis was forced to retreat from his victory to Wilmington, North Carolina. From there, having received supplies and reinforcements by sea, he embarked on a fateful march north, into Virginia.

Affairs in Virginia had gone disastrously for the rebel cause. Benedict Arnold, now a general in British employ, had invaded the state in January 1781 with a force of nearly 2,000 loyalist volunteers. He met little organized resistance and had the pleasure of chasing Virginia's governor, Thomas Jefferson, from Richmond with the greatest ease. Washington sent Lafayette south with a small detachment to handle Arnold. But the marquis, lacking naval support, could accomplish nothing in that land of broad tidal rivers.

Cornwallis started north from Wilmington, North Carolina, late in April 1781. Marching unopposed into Virginia, he joined forces with Arnold's men (now commanded by British general William Phillips) and received further reinforcements from Sir Henry Clinton in New York. This brought Cornwallis's numbers to 7,200. Brushing aside Lafayette's small detachment, he marched his troops into the small port of Yorktown on Chesapeake Bay and began converting it into a permanent military and naval base. From this "Gibraltar of America" he planned to strike out into the interior, capture all of Virginia, and then turn north for that final campaign, in conjunction with Clinton's army, which should finish off the rebellion once and for all. But while he busily fortified York-town, the elements of a vast and far-flung operation against him were being assembled.

The decisive factors in the Yorktown campaign were not to be American; they were to be French. The idea that Corn-wallis might have placed himself in a trap first occurred to Lafayette. That young officer realized that the elements for a great combination might be at hand. There was Washington's army still encamped at White Plains; there was Comte de Rochambeau's French expeditionary force (sent over in re-sponse to Lafayette's pleadings at the French court) of 6,000 men, which had seized Newport, Rhode Island, in 1780 and been holed up there ever since; and there was a French fleet in the West Indies, playing blindman's buff against an English squadron. If all of these forces could be coordinated and brought to bear against Cornwallis, something decisive might, at long last, be accomplished. Hurrying north, Lafayette urged Washington to initiate combined operations against the British in Virginia.

Washington, whose gaze had been fixed upon Sir Henry Clinton's army in New York, was, at first, reluctant. His plans called for an assault on New York City. But, of course, either attack would depend entirely upon command of the sea. "In any operation, and under all circumstances," he wrote to Rochambeau, "a decisive Naval superiority is to be considered as a fundamental principle, and the basis upon which every hope of success must ultimately depend." Therefore he agreed with Rochambeau and Lafayette that the point of military at-tack would depend upon whatever target was chosen by the French fleet.

That fleet, under the command of the great French ad-miral, Comte de Grasse, having captured an island or two from the British, had convoyed a fleet of 200 merchantmen to Saint-Domingue. It now took aboard 3,000 French soldiers of the garrison and headed north—partly to escape the Caribbean hurricane season but mainly in response to pleas from Rochambeau. De Grasse, remembering Admiral d'Estaing's failure to break through the Narrows into New York Harbor three years earlier, decided upon Yorktown as the proper target. His large fleet (including twenty-four ships of the line, the battleships of their day) would have more room to maneuver in Chesapeake Bay.

Late in July, Rochambeau began withdrawing his army from Newport to join forces with Washington at White Plains. There, on August 12, the two commanders received de Grasse's dispatch informing them that Yorktown, and not New York, would be their objective. Leaving behind 4,000 men to mislead Sir Henry Clinton into thinking nothing was afoot, Washington and Rochambeau began to slip their combined armies south on August 19, 1781. By August 31 they were marching through Philadelphia. Everything now depended on whether de Grasse could keep the British fleet out of Chesapeake Bay long enough for the Franco-American forces to surround Cornwallis at Yorktown.

On September 2, Washington wrote to Lafayette: "I am distressed beyond expression, to know what is become of the Count de Grasse, and for fear the English fleet, by occupying the Chesapeake . . . should frustrate all our flattering prospects in that quarter." Three days later, while his men were marching through Chester, Pennsylvania, Washington received news that de Grasse's fleet was in the Chesapeake. The French officer who brought the dispatch reported that "Washington acted like a child whose every wish has been gratified."

And at that very moment, on September 5, 1781, the decisive naval battle of the war was being fought off the capes of the Chesapeake. For the British, tardy as usual, had finally arrived. A fleet of nineteen ships of the line, under the command of Admiral Thomas Graves, bore down on the French line of battle, decks cleared for action, the royal ensign fluttering defiantly at every masthead. The British were outnumbered—but the Royal Navy was used to fighting and beating French or Spanish fleets no matter what the odds. However, on this occasion they were not only overgunned but outmaneuvered by the cunning de Grasse. After two hours of flaming battle two British ships of the line were in sinking condition and the rest badly damaged, while the French ships were barely scratched. The battle off the Chesapeake capes was one of the few in which the Royal Navy was ever beaten by the French. But for the rebel cause in North America it was decisive. While Admiral Graves led his limping squadron back to New York for refitting and repairs, Admiral de Grasse's ships sailed into the York River, cutting the British off from all means of supply and any hope of escape.

Three weeks later, on September 28, the French and American armies of Rochambeau and Washington began digging in across the neck of the Yorktown peninsula, and Cornwallis was under siege. He had some 8,000 men under his command inside the little town. The French forces of Rochambeau and Saint-Simon numbered nearly as many, while Washington had 5,645 Continentals and 3,200 Virginia militiamen with him. The siege, which was conducted along formal military lines, lasted less than a month. Casualties were few on either side, but Cornwallis was soldier enough to recognize the hopelessness of his position. On October 19, 1781, he surrendered himself and his entire army to the allies. The British regulars glumly marched out of Yorktown between two lines of French and Continental soldiers while the English regimental bands played a popular tune of the day entitled, "The World Turned Upside Down." Although the victory had been almost exclusively French, Rochambeau, with typical generosity, insisted that the British commander make his formal surrender to Washington.

When, on November 25, Lord North received the news of Yorktown in London, he threw up his arms and staggered as though he'd been hit in the breast by a musket ball. "O God!" he cried, "it is all over!" But at first glance it is difficult to tell why he thought so. True, a second British army had been swallowed whole by the rebels. But British forces still occupied New York in large numbers, as well as Charleston, Savannah, and other important coastal towns. Furthermore, they enjoyed almost complete control of the Ohio Valley and the American west. And although a British squadron had been defeated in battle, the Royal Navy could still dominate any waters it chose to concentrate in.

Why, then, did Lord North immediately assume that Yorktown spelled utter defeat for Britain's attempt to subdue the American rebellion? Because Lord North, for all his failings, was an experienced politician—with a politician's nose for trouble. The war against the Americans had never aroused much enthusiasm in England. It was there, as it was in America, a rich man's quarrel and a poor man's fight. But now, faced with steeply mounting taxation and no discernible end to the fighting in sight, the discouraging news from Virginia was that last ounce of despair which tilted the scales of British self-interest. The English ruling class of 1781 reached the same conclusion that other ruling classes have reached in our own day when faced with endless national liberation struggles in such places as Palestine, India, Algeria, Vietnam, and various African colonies—future profits could not match present losses.

Accordingly, there was a changing of the guard in London. Lord North had been begging his sovereign to allow him to retire; Yorktown finally convinced the reluctant king. In March 1782, George III was forced to accept a new ministry composed of his detested enemies, the liberal Whigs, including Charles Fox. That opened the way for peace negotiations.

Vergennes, worried lest his American allies abandon the struggle while France was still fighting, persuaded Congress to order its envoys in Paris to negotiate with Britain only under French direction. Congress agreed and dispatched John Jay and John Adams to France to help Benjamin Franklin deal with the British commissioners. Franklin, of course, paid little heed to Congress's humiliating instructions. He dealt with the British without consulting Vergennes. The shrewd old philosopher drove a hard bargain and gained more than Congress had any right to expect.

By the terms of the preliminary peace treaty signed between Britain and the United States on November 30, 1782, the new nation won a truly imperial domain—west to the Mississippi, north to the St. Lawrence–Great Lakes boundary, south to the Floridas. At the insistence of the Bostonian, Adams, the British even agreed to preserve the ancient privilege of New England fishermen to land and dry their catch on the Newfoundland coast. In return for all this the Americans agreed to pay any outstanding debts owed to British merchants, and Congress promised to "earnestly recommend" to the various states that they restore confiscated property to the unfortunate loyalists.

All of this was confirmed in the final peace treaty signed with Great Britain by the United States, France, Spain, and the Netherlands in Paris on September 3, 1783. The French, who had done so much to win the victory, received but little at the peace table—the West Indian island of Tobago and the colony of Senegal in Africa. Vergennes would probably have done better but for the fact that a British fleet had defeated (and captured) Admiral de Grasse in the Caribbean "Battle of the Saints" early in April 1782. The Spaniards, who had done almost nothing during the war, received the Floridas and the Mediterranean island of Minorca but failed to win back Gibraltar, which had been their principal war aim.

The new republic was hailed with enthusiasm by English liberals, who felt that the American victory had saved them from an approaching royal despotism at home. However doubtful that might have been, it is certain that no English monarch ever again aspired to the kind of power exercised by George III between 1774 and 1782. As for the English Tories, they confidently predicted that the Americans would soon come crawling back to the imperial fold. It was to take yet another struggle—the naval War of 1812—to convince them that the United States had arrived to stay among the family of nations. The French intelligentsia and radical bourgeoisie cheered what they considered to be the victory of liberty over autocracy, and prepared to ignite the same kind of explosion in their own country. It was only when the United States refused to come to the aid of the revolutionary French Republic that these same intellectuals and radicals began to apprehend that the American struggle had not, perhaps, represented a truly revolutionary movement.

But Europeans accepted the rebel propaganda evaluation of their victory at face value and felt that it signaled the dawn of a better day in the Old World as well as the New. And, since the Word is, in almost every case, mightier than the Fact, they were right. As the British historian Lord Acton observed: "It was from America that the plain ideas that men ought to mind their own business, and that the nation is responsible to Heaven for the acts of the State . . . burst forth like a conqueror upon the world they were destined to transform, under the title of the Rights of Man . . . and the principle gained ground, that *a nation can never abandon its fate to an authority it cannot control.*"

News of the peace treaty (which included an immediate cease-fire) reached North America on March 12, 1783, and so, to the "inexpressible satisfaction" of General Washington, the fighting stopped. Recently, by a personal appeal to his men, the general had barely prevented the Continental Army from marching on Philadelphia to force Congress to pay them at sword's point. The hapless Congress was so destitute that, in the end, the soldiers had to be sent home without pay, only IOUs signed personally by Robert Morris. But they were allowed to keep their muskets as a gift.

Meantime, Cornwallis's defeat at Yorktown had already forced the British evacuation of Charleston, Wilmington, and Savannah in 1782. The departing transports carried not only regulars, but many thousands of former black slaves now embarked as free men and many thousands of loyalists fleeing certain rebel vengeance. The British army in New York (now commanded by Sir Guy Carleton) sailed away from that city on November 25, 1783—and, again, their departure was the signal for a mass exodus by thousands of loyalists. Many of these were to settle in Canada, especially at St. John in New Brunswick and along the Newfoundland coast. Since their ranks included so many of the better educated class of Americans, their departure struck a blow to native culture from which it was a generation in recovering.

The departing British could do little, of course, for their Indian allies in the west. These were now exposed to the full fury of that American policy of genocide which, within a century, would utterly extinguish their culture and come close to wiping out their entire race.

As for the triumphant rebels, on the morrow of victory they raised their heads in the sudden silence and realized that somehow, impossibly, against all the odds, they had won. Not only had they won, they had won on their own terms. For, as we have seen, the basic idea of almost all the rebel leaders (with the possible exception of Sam Adams, Thomas Paine, and a few others) had been to establish American independence with *as little social and economic upheaval* as possible— to win a rebellion without igniting a real revolution. And in this they were largely successful. For the new American republic of which they were now to be the architects and whose destinies they were to guide for a generation was but little different in its social and economic manifestations from the colonial society it replaced.

Yet in order to enlist that bare minimum of support essential to their victory, American leaders had filled the air with propaganda and promises—and these proved in the long run to be self-fulfilling. For if the American War of National Liberation (which is what such a struggle would be called today) produced no real revolution in American society, it bequeathed to that society and to the world explosively revolutionary ideas. The political structure erected by the rebel leaders a few years later in Philadelphia at the Constitutional Convention of 1787 was indeed something new under the sun. Although designed to preserve an existing social and economic order, the Constitution, like the Declaration of Independence, embodied the *promise,* if not the fact, of true democracy, true equality, and even true brotherhood for all men. But these were promises which later generations of Americans would have to fight to fulfill—and the end of that struggle is not yet in sight.

# EPILOGUE | "I Cannot Come to Each of You..."

"... The time now drew near when the Commander-in-Chief intended to leave this part of the country for his beloved retreat at Mount Vernon. On Tuesday, the 4th of December, it was made known to the officers then in New York, that General Washington intended to commence his journey that day.

"At 12 o'clock the officers repaired to Fraunces' Tavern, in Pearl Street, where General Washington had appointed to meet them, and to take his final leave of them. We had been assembled but a few moments, when His Excellency entered the room. His emotion, too strong to be concealed, seemed to be reciprocated by every officer present.

"After partaking of a slight refreshment, in almost breathless silence, the General filled his glass with wine, and turning to the officers said, 'With a heart full of love and gratitude, I now take leave of you. I most devoutly wish that your latter days may be as prosperous and happy as your former ones have been glorious and honorable.'

"After the officers had taken a glass of wine, General Washington said, 'I cannot come to each of you, but shall feel obliged if each of you will come and take me by the hand.'

"General Knox, being nearest to him, turned to his Commander-in-Chief, who, suffused in tears, was incapable of utterance, but grasped his hand; then they embraced each other in silence. In the same affectionate manner, every officer in the room marched up to, kissed, and parted with his Commander-in-Chief. Such a scene of sorrow and weeping I have never before witnessed, and hope I may never be called upon to witness again. It was indeed too affecting to be of long continuance, for tears of sensibility filled every eye, and the heart seemed so full, that it was ready to burst from its wonted abode. Not a word was uttered to break the solemn silence that prevailed, or to interrupt the tenderness of that interesting scene. The simple thought that we were then about to part from the man who had conducted us through a long and bloody war, and under whose conduct the glory and independence of our country had been achieved . . . seemed to me utterly insupportable.

"But the time of separation had come, and waving his hand to his grieving children around him, he left the room and passing through a corps of light infantry who were paraded to receive him, he walked silently to Whitehall, where a barge was waiting. We all followed in mournful silence to the wharf, where a prodigious crowd had assembled to witness the departure of the man who, under God, had been the great agent in establishing the glory and independence of these United States. As soon as he was seated, the barge put off into the river, and when out in the stream, our great and beloved General waved his hat, and bid us a silent adieu. We paid him the same compliment."

Lt. Colonel Benjamin Tallmadge
Continental Army

# Bibliography

Abernethy, T. P. *Western Lands and the American Revolution*. Charlottesville, 1937.

Adams, Charles Francis, ed. *Familiar Letters of John Adams and His Wife, Abigail Adams, during the Revolution*. New York, 1876.

Adams, James Truslow. *The Founding of New England*. Boston, 1921.

Adams, John. *Diary and Autobiography of John Adams*. New York, 1964.

Alden, John R. *A History of the American Revolution*. New York, 1969.

Alt-Lossberg. *Journal of the Honorable Fusilier von Alt-Lossberg*. Morristown National Historical Park.

Andrews, Charles M. *The Colonial Period of American History*. New Haven, 1938.

Bancroft, George. *History of the United States*. Boston, 1874.

Beard, Charles and Mary. *The Rise of American Civilization*. New York, 1930.

Becker, Carl L. *The Eve of the Revolution*. New Haven, 1921.

Bemis, Samuel F. *The Diplomacy of the American Revolution*. New York, 1935.

Bill, A. H. *Valley Forge: The Making of an Army*. New York, 1952.

Boatner, Mark Mayo. *Encyclopedia of the American Revolution*. New York, 1966.

Brady, Alexander. *Democracy in the Dominions*. London, 1953.

Brebner, J. B. *North Atlantic Triangle: The Interplay of Canada, the United States, and Great Britain*. New Haven, 1945.

Brinton, Crane. *The Anatomy of Revolution*. New York, 1951.

Burnett, Edmund. *The Continental Congress*. New York, 1964.

Chase, Ellen. *The Beginnings of the American Revolution*. New York, 1910.

Coleman, R. V. *Liberty and Property*. New York, 1951.

Coupland, Reginald. *The American Revolution and the British Empire*. London, 1930.

Davidson, Philip. *Propaganda and the American Revolution*. New York, 1973.

Donoughue, Bernard. *British Politics and the American Revolution*. London, 1964.

Dorn, Walter L. *Competition for Empire*. New York, 1940.

Egerton, H. E. *The Causes and Character of the American Revolution*. Oxford, 1923.

Fast, Howard, ed. *The Selected Works of Tom Paine*. New York, 1945.

Flexner, James T. *George Washington: The Forge of Experience*. Boston, 1965.

————. *George Washington in the American Revolution*. Boston, 1967.

Freeman, Douglas Southall. *George Washington*. New York, 1954.

Gipson, Lawrence Henry. *The Coming of the Revolution*. New York, 1954.

Gottschalk, Louis. *Lafayette and the Close of the American Revolution*. Chicago, 1942.

Greene, Evarts B. *The Foundations of American Nationality*. New York, 1968.

————. *The Revolutionary Generation*. New York, 1943.

Guttridge, G. H. *English Whiggism and the American Revolution*. Berkeley, 1942.

Harlow, V. T. *The Founding of the Second British Empire*. London, 1952.

Harper, L. A. *The English Navigation Laws*. New York, 1939.

Hunt, William. *The History of England*. London, 1905.

Jameson, J. Franklin. *The American Revolution Considered as a Social Movement*. Princeton, 1969.

Keith, A. B. *Constitutional History of the First British Empire.* Oxford, 1930.

Labaree, Benjamin Woods. *The Boston Tea Party.* New York, 1966.

Labaree, Leonard W. *Royal Government in America.* New Haven, 1930.

Lloyd, Alan. *The King Who Lost America.* New York, 1971.

Mahan, A. T. *The Influence of Sea Power upon History.* Boston, 1902.

Miller, John C. *Triumph of Freedom.* Boston, 1948.

―――. *Sam Adams: Pioneer in Propaganda.* Boston, 1936.

Montross, Lynn. *The Reluctant Rebels.* New York, 1950.

Moore, Frank. *The Diary of the American Revolution.* New York, 1967.

Morris, Richard B. *The American Revolution Reconsidered.* New York, 1967.

―――. *Seven Who Shaped Our Destiny.* New York, 1973.

Namier, L. B. *England in the Age of the American Revolution.* London, 1930.

Nettels, Curtis B. *George Washington and American Independence.* Boston, 1951.

Nevins, Allan. *The American States during and after the Revolution.* New York, 1924.

Osgood, H. L. *The American Colonies in the Eighteenth Century.* New York, 1924.

Pares, R. *King George III and the Politicians.* Oxford, 1953.

Parkman, Francis. *A Half Century of Conflict.* Boston, 1929.

―――. *Montcalm and Wolfe.* Boston, 1927.

Parrington, Vernon L. *Main Currents in American Thought.* New York, 1930.

Pearson, Michael. *Those Damned Rebels: The American Revolution as Seen through British Eyes.* New York, 1972.

Rankin, Hugh F. *The American Revolution.* New York, 1965.

Robson, Eric. *The American Revolution in Its Political and Military Aspects.* New York, 1972.

Rossiter, Clinton. *The First American Revolution.* New York, 1956.

Sabine, Lorenzo. *The American Loyalists.* Boston, 1847.

Schlesinger, Arthur M. *The Colonial Merchants and the American Revolution.* New York, 1918.

Smith, Justin H. *Our Struggle for the Fourteenth Colony*. New York, 1907.

Sparks, Jared, ed. *Correspondence of the American Revolution*. Boston, 1853.

Stark, J. H. *The Loyalists of Massachusetts*. Boston, 1910.

Swiggett, Howard. *The Extraordinary Mister Morris*. New York, 1952.

Thatcher, Oxenbridge. *Sentiments of a British American*. Boston, 1764.

Trevelyan, George O. *The American Revolution*. London, 1928.

Van Doren, Carl, ed. *Letters and Papers of Benjamin Franklin and Richard Jackson*. Philadelphia, 1941.

Van Tyne, C. H. *England and America*. Cambridge, 1927.

Walpole, Horace. *Journal of the Reign of King George the Third*. London, 1859.

———. *Letters*. Oxford, 1905.

Wickwire, Franklin and Mary. *Cornwallis: The American Adventure*. Boston, 1970.

Wilkin, W. H. *Some British Soldiers in America*. London, 1914.

Wortley, E. Stuart. *A Prime Minister and His Son*. London, 1925.

*The Dictionary of American Biography*. New York, 1936.

*The Dictionary of National Biography*. London, 1885.

# SUGGESTED READING

*The Diplomacy of the American Revolution* (New York, 1935), by Samuel Flagg Bemis, is still the best account of the serpentine maneuverings of Franklin, Deane, Vergennes, Floridablanca, *et al.* as they tried to use common means to very different ends.

*The Winter Soldiers* (New York, 1975), by Richard Ketchum, is a very well-written, fast-paced, yet thoughtful account of the sufferings of the Continental Army up to the end of the New Jersey campaign.

*The Boston Tea Party* (New York, 1966), by Benjamin Woods Labaree, is a fascinatingly intimate account of the strange doings in Massachusetts which culminated in that fateful nonsense in Boston Harbor.

*Triumph of Freedom* (Boston, 1948), by John C. Miller, is a highly readable one-volume account of the Revolution in all its aspects.

*Montcalm and Wolfe* (Boston, 1927), by Francis Parkman, is the classic account of the Seven Years' War by one of the greatest of American historians.

*The American Revolution* (New York, 1965), by Hugh F. Rankin, is a very well-edited collection of eyewitness accounts with a readable and intelligent commentary.

*The Devil's Disciple,* by George Bernard Shaw, is the bitingly hilarious play based on the misadventures of "Gentleman Johnny" Burgoyne in the American wilderness.

# Index

*Italic* number indicates illustration.

MJ